THE WHOLEGRAIN OVEN

PL 361413   BIN 1113E   SHOP LS

LEAMINGTON SPA   A/N/CO FLAM PB   £4.50   ISBN 0572013841

WHOLEGRAIN OVEN   CONIL/CONIL

24/09/87

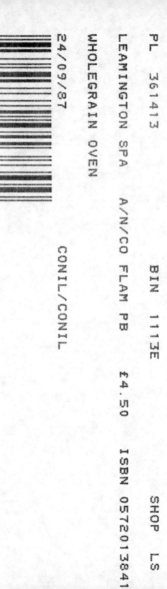

THE WHOLEGRAIN OVEN

Christopher &
Jean Conil

W. Foulsham & Co. Ltd.
London ● New York ● Toronto ● Cape Town ● Sydney

W. Foulsham & Company Limited
Yeovil Road, Slough, Berkshire,
SL1 4JH

ISBN 0–572–01384–1

Printed in Spain by Cayfosa, Barcelona
Dep. leg. B-27224-1986

CONTENTS

ACKNOWLEDGEMENTS

To my father Jean Conil, whose scrutiny ensured that every detail was carefully checked. To my wife Suzanne, whose patience over the keyboard maintained a steady flow of words. Chris Newman and Mike Ward for their making and baking, and the Breadwinners who tried and tested every loaf. Also acknowledgement is due to Marriages & Son Ltd. for their kind support and for the use of their products.

I should also like to thank Gordon Shepherd of the Southend-on-Sea Technical College Photographic Department and his assistants for all their work on the photographs.

Christopher Conil

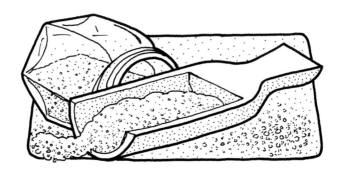

THE AUTHOR

Master Baker Christopher Conil following his father Master Chef Jean Conil into catering, Christopher decided to concentrate on the crusty side of the industry and after many years training in some of London's most prestigious establishments, graduated in Baking and Food Technology at the National Bakery School.

With the growing trend towards natural food, Christopher and his wife Suzanne opened their first Hot Bread Kitchen in Southend-on-Sea. Christopher is well known in his local area for his appearances on radio and his lectures and demonstrations on baking.

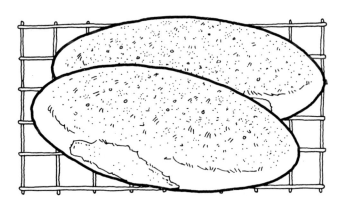

INTRODUCTION

Over the past 20 years I have experienced many changes in the baking industry. Some have benefited the craftsman, some have not. The growth in health foods, namely breads with high fibre are increasing in popularity, the range is extending daily.

My book includes bread and Danish confectionery recipes which are tried, tested and produced in Southend. We supply many health food shops who are eager to try new lines. My bakery business extends into promotions, demonstrations and talks on all aspects of bread and flour confectionery to Womens Institutes and local radio. For many years I have been involved in the commercial manufacturing of bread and confectionery, and have followed many fads in food eating, but none has lasted as long as the present one, which is now becoming a way of life.

I am now realising that wholemeal, honey, dried fruits, yoghurt, low poly-unsaturated fats and all the natural untampered foods we use to make our products, are now becoming accepted as being a replacement for white flour, sugar, animal fats, synthetic colours, preservatives, additives and oxidents etc. The demand is growing for new, tasty and healthy products to eat. Recently we introduced a herb loaf, different in that all the ingredients were as natural and organically grown as we could get. The sales of these and other similar products has increased dramatically. There is now an awareness for an alternative to convenience foods.

In this book I intend to show you how different the taste of natural ingredients can be when put together in varying quantities. All the recipes have been tried on our customers with high recommendations, which just proves that the "proof of the pudding is in the eating."!

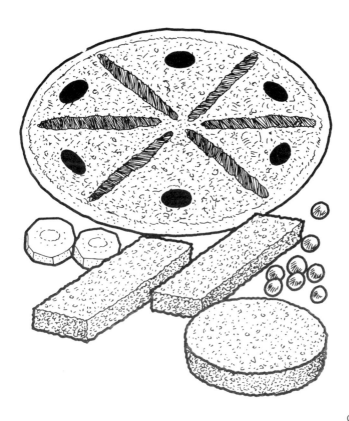

THE TREND TOWARDS WHOLEMEAL BREAD

Breadmaking has been with us for many years. Since the early Egyptians, man has toiled with the idea of producing the best bread using simple practices, but lacking in the necessary technology, had been unable to overcome the problems we now face. Today breadmaking has become more sophisticated. Bread can be produced untouched by human hand. Wholemeal bread has increased in popularity, as have many speciality and 100 per cent grain loaves. We're all talking about high fibre foods, but wholemeal bread has always been here!

Wholemeal bread consumption has shown a sharp increase over the last five years. A government national food survey shows an increase from 2.01 oz per person per week in 1981 to 6.08 oz in 1984.

Ounces per person per week

	1981	1982	1983	1984
Wholemeal/wholewheat	2.01	2.08	2.17	6.08
White	21.93	21.70	20.81	20.45

As you can see, white bread is in decline, which proves that wholemeal and other natural high fibre flours are being included in many other products than just bread. Major manufacturers are launching new health products all the time. Wholemeal bread itself is now bought by 60 per cent of housewives every week.

INGREDIENTS

The quality of finished bread is determined by the type of ingredients and method used. For the best results there are a few points to bear in mind.

FLOURS

Wholemeal flour is the main ingredient in making good wholemeal bread. Other flours are available and are widely used in the baking industry. Sometimes, however, a new flour comes on the market which creates a lot of interest. These are proprietary flours for speciality breads. Wholemeal flour consists of the whole of the wheat, milled by stone or roller mills.

Stoneground is generally coarser than roller milled and will absorb more water. The method releases oil in the germ, which can, if stored for too long, produce 'off' flavours. Wholemeal is excellent as part of a healthy diet, the fibre being essential for prevention of constipation and other digestive complaints.

Wheatmeal is flour milled to a more refined state (usually 85-90 per cent of the wholewheat. The result is a flour that is ideal for bread and confectionery which requires a lighter consistency. The flavour is not so strong as wholemeal flour. Make sure it is free of additives and grown organically.

11

Malted grain (granary) is increasing in popularity. It has the addition of malted grains which require strong teeth to eat! The malted grains impart a particular flavour that is unique to this type of bread.

Hovis conjures up images of old-time bakers running for miles up cobbled streets delivering bread. Hovi's flavour is of brown bread with a difference — its light, fine textured and with a hint of nuttiness. It has extra salt and germ of the grain added to the basic wheatmeal flour to add to the nutritional value.

Rye flour is certain to become as popular as wholemeal in the near future. In other parts of Europe it is one of the main ingredients in all types of rye bread, pumpernickel, rusks, biscuits, etc. It is darker in colour and feels gritty. It is low in gluten and therefore, when baked, is quite heavy. In Britain we use a half rye and half flour to give a lighter touch and the flavour is enhanced with carraway seeds added to the dough.

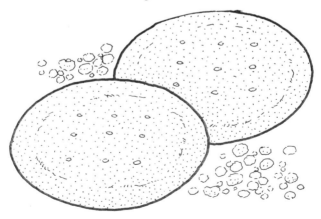

OTHER GRAINS AND MEALS

Cornmeal:
The flour of maize, corn bread, corn pancakes and other traditional morsels are made from this meal.
Buckwheat: used in batters for pancakes and also in bread.
Oats: mainly used in porridge, muesli and oatcakes, etc.
Bran: source of extra fibre in cereals, bread, etc.
Wheatgerm: mainly in Hovis but also in cereals.
Malt flour: used to impart richness and sugar to bread and cakes.

SUGARS

Raw sugar: unrefined with some of the natural minerals present.
Honey: natural sugars used to sweeten many foods.
Dark brown sugar: used in bread and confectionery adding a rich colouring.
Demerara sugar: lighter in colour than dark brown and also more refined.
Fruit sugar: natural and unrefined; not so sweet as cane sugars.
Muscovado: different degrees of refinement.
Molasses (raw sugar syrup): used to colour and sweeten rich malt bread, etc.
Treacle: a bitter-sweet syrup ideal for ginger goods — parkin, toffees, etc.
Golden syrups: a light syrup used for cakes and puddings.

FATS AND OILS

These are necessary in breads and yeast goods for richness, shortness, volume, colour and storage qualities. Only vegetable fats and oils should be used, as these are low in polyunsaturates and are a great benefit in healthy eating.

Fats used:
Vegetable margarines
Sunflower oil
Olive oil
White shortenings
Corn oil
Nut oils

YEAST

Yeast is the essential rising agent in the fermentation process. Yeast converts sugars in the dough mainly from the starches in the flour to carbon dioxide (gas) and alcohol. The alcohol evaporates on baking. The gas expands the dough, which stretches the glutenous structure and develops a cellular appearance, giving the characteristic volume associated with well baked bread.

Other changes take place in baking which impart a delicate crust, colour and flavour. Like wine bread flavour develops in long fermentation times or 'proving'. An alternative method much used today is the use of ascorbic acid to speed up fermentation. Used carefully it produces an acceptable loaf.

Yeast can be bought either dried or compressed, the latter being more suitable as it is activated quickly in the dough. Yeast contains 75 per cent water and is therefore highly perishable. For this reason it should be refrigerated. It will keep for at least a week. Dried yeast works in the same way but needs longer to activate in water. Time should be allowed before mixing the other ingredients. One tip. Do not mix salt with yeast as it will kill the rising powers and the bread will be flat and unpalatable. Try the new dried active yeast with Vitamin C. Just mix into the flour and make as normal. No fermentation needed, just prove in the tins and bake. Use a sachet per 750g/1½lb of strong flour. All the recipes in this book are based on using fresh, compressed yeast. If using dried yeast adjust the weight to allow for this and use about half the stated weight.

SALT

Salt is added for flavour and to develop other flavours present in foods. Always mix salt into the flour as it will inhibit the action of the yeast. About $15g/\frac{1}{2}oz$ per quart of liquor for bun and sweet goods, slightly more for bread.

MILK POWDERS

Whey powder and skimmed milk are used to increase the food value, improve the crumb texture and richness of baked products. Milk bread should contain 6 per cent whole milk solids. Butter milk is used in Irish Soda bread which uses bicarbonate of soda as the aeration. This is called lactic fermentation. The bicarbonate of soda reacts with the buttermilk to produce carbon dioxide which aerates the dough.

EGGS

Free-range are used to enrich and colour yeast-raised doughs. It also increases volume, and as a glaze for the tops of crusts.

NATURAL ADDITIVES

These are malt extract, malt flours and soya flours. These are added to improve the overall appearance and natural flavour of baked goods. The best free additive is T.L.C. - Tender Loving Care!

16

FLAVOURS AND SPICES

Care should be taken when adding flavours and spices as these can retard the yeast activity if used too liberally. Always mix spices into fruits as this disperses the flavour throughout the mix. Vanilla, lemon, orange and almond are most often used.

SPICES

Use nutmeg, mixed spice, ginger, etc.

EQUIPMENT

The main equipment is a good pair of hands or better still an electric mixer will eliminate a lot of time and develop the dough better. A rolling pin, a thermometer, a sharp knife, a baking sheet and tins, a pastry brush, 1 litre/2 pint measuring jug, a set of accurate scales.

FRUIT AND NUTS

A wide selection is now available in the high street, from the bitter-sweet almonds to the more exotic pistachio nut. Since early biblical times, nuts have been cultivated from middle eastern countries where its growth has spread to Greece and many parts of the world. Rich in protein, Vitamin B and minerals like calcium, iron and phosphorus, nuts are a natural and healthy additive which enriches any bread or confection. Some of the most popular ones are almonds, hazelnuts, walnuts, peanuts, cashews, brazils and coconuts.

FRUITS

Dried fruits are used extensively in the baking trade, but only the more popular ones — sultanas, currants, cherries and mixed peel. Try also dried apricots, high in Vitamins A, B and C; dates — rich in natural carbohydrates which are easily digested and combined with nuts and seeds and makes a great difference when added to fruit bun loaves; figs are ideal in a muesli loaf; prunes are high in mineral content and vitamins, used in French custard flans. Others to experiment with are raisins, peaches, apples and bananas.

SEEDS

These are increasingly being used in breads and confectionery, the health-giving qualities enhance the natural taste of any food. Sesame seeds are white in appearance and are used on top or mixed in with the dough of many different types of bread. They impart a very special flavour. Poppy or maw seeds are a traditional topping on bloomer loaves, but are also used in combination with nuts and honey to make a far eastern filling. Carraway seeds have a strong flavour and you can include them when making rye bread. Other seeds include sunflower and pumpkin.

THE ART AND CRAFT OF BREADMAKING

The secret of good breadmaking is to understand what happens when strong flour, salt, yeast and water are joined together. A good loaf is one, when the correct ingredients in the right proportion are blended and manipulated to the right degree, fermented to the right maturity and baked to the right time and temperature. Then it will be received with the right appreciation.

Use fresh yeast as it works faster than dried yeast. Remember that yeast is a living micro-organism and should be treated with care. Dissolve it in warm water between 76–80°F/30–40°C. Dried yeast will keep for many months and can be treated the same as fresh yeast when it is mixed with warm water and a little sugar.

When mixing dough by hand be sure to knead it well. The palm of the hand should push the dough continually over and over for at least 15 minutes. It's hard work but that is how bread used to be made. Use your electric mixer for speed but make sure you mix it for at least 5–15 minutes or until the dough is smooth and elastic. The finished dough temperature should be about 78–82°F/26°C to produce satisfactory results. Ascorbic acid tablets can be used in all the recipes to eliminate the fermentation process. It acts on the gluten, conferring the necessary development a dough requires. Use 1 tablet for each mixing.

The traditional method produces a loaf that imparts a natural fermented flavour – but only time will tell. When the dough is ready for placing in the tins it should be weighed into 450/900g or 1/2 lb loaves and shaped into long sausages. Be sure to put the seam end at the bottom of the tin otherwise it will blow open during baking, leaving what we call a cauliflower top. Be sure to grease the tins first.

During the final prove just before baking, the loaf should be placed in a warm humid atmosphere and covered with an oily polythene sheet. Just when the loaf appears above the top of the tin — after about 40/50 minutes — it is time to bake. Cut the top as for a split tin. The oven should be preheated to 230°C/450°F/Gas Mark 8. Make sure the top of the loaf does not dry or skin before baking, otherwise the loaf will not rise satisfactorily when baked, producing an uneven shape which is not desired.

With care and attention a loaf can be made as well as any Master Baker!

BREADMAKING TIPS

1. Make sure all ingredients are of the highest quality, i.e. 100 per cent strong wholemeal flour, fresh yeast, warm water, sea salt. Soft flour is not good for making bread.

2. All the baking tins should be warm and well greased. New tins should be baked 'blind' before using otherwise the dough will take longer in the final prove and there is a danger of sticking.

3. Do not mix yeast with salt as it will kill all the micro-organisms which produce good bread.

4. To speed up fermentation use a 25mg tablet of ascorbic acid per mixing.

5. If you use dried yeast dissolve it beforehand with a little sugar. Dried yeast will keep longer than fresh, which will keep for a few days in the fridge.

6. Be as accurate as you can when weighing out the ingredients. The water content may vary depending on the type of flour used. Wholemeal will absorb more water than white flour.

7. Fat added to the recipe will give a loaf with a softer crumb, less prone to go stale and more pleasant to eat.

8. In our bakery in Southend we use a special cabinet for the final prove. If you would like to make up a similar device then place a bowl of warm water into the bottom of your oven which should only be just warm enough otherwise the dough will bake. The water vaporises, producing a suitable environment for proving the dough. Then remove this dough for 10 minutes until the oven reaches 230°C/450°F/Gas Mark 8. Leave the water in to create a steamy atmosphere for final baking.

9. Place loaf in the oven. After 10 minutes remove the bowl of water and continue baking for about 30–40 minutes. It should sound hollow when fully baked. The result should be a loaf with a golden crust, well proved with a soft crumb that tastes like the bread that grandma used to make. If, after all this you still have problems then I should buy a loaf from your local Master Baker — and let him do

all the hard work! Still, keep trying — it can be great fun.

10. Always sieve the flour. This aerates and disperses other ingredients quicker. Any dough left over you can turn into rolls about 50g/2oz each or fancy breads, knotted, torpedo, cottage, batons, etc. Pizzas make an ideal snack using any spare dough to produce the base, then freeze it for another day.

11. Fermentation is controlled by temperature and the amount of yeast used. Always keep everything warm while making bread. The kitchen itself should be around 70°F/21°C and the dough temperature about 80°F/27°C to ensure good fermentation.

Temperature of water: 80°F/27°C × 2 = 160°F/55°C subtract the flour temp 70°F/21°C. Temperature of water: 90°F/32°C produces a dough temp of 80°F/27°C.

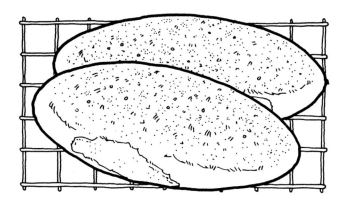

1. Bread Basics

COUNTRY WHOLEMEAL BREAD

A classic amongst healthy breads — all the grain is used to make a 100 per cent flour which has a strong nutty flavour with extra fibre. This recipe also has extra goodness in the form of cracked wheat.

INGREDIENTS	Metric	Imperial	American
Wholemeal flour	800g	1 lb 12oz	7 cups
Salt	2 tsp	2 tsp	2 tsp
Malt extract	2 tsp	2 tsp	2 tsp
Yeast	2 tsp	2 tsp	2 tsp
Water	550ml	1 pint	2½ cups
Ascorbic acid tablet	25mg	25mg	25mg
Cracked wheat	25g	1oz	2 tbsp
Vegetable fat	25g	1oz	2 tbsp

1 Mix together the flour, salt and malt extract in a bowl and add the fat.

2 Mix the yeast in a little warm water and add this to the other ingredients. Add the remaining water and mix to a clear dough using a mixer for about 5 minutes. This can be done by hand but will take 15 minutes kneading. It is very important to knead well.

3 If using the ascorbic acid tablet then the dough will be ready for weighing into warm tins or trays after 10 minutes 'rest'. Using the traditional method (without ascorbic acid) leave to ferment in a warm place for 1 hour, using a knock back at 40 minutes. This means the dough should be kneaded again and deflated of the bubbles thus returning it to its solid state.

4 Weigh the dough into 450g/1 lb loaves and into trays for baking. You can use large trays for the traditional cottage loaf, or weigh the dough into 2oz/50g rounds to bake into rolls.

5 Leave the dough to 'prove' for approximately 40 minutes or until double in volume. Make sure the top is moist by using an egg wash (an egg well beaten). Sprinkle cracked wheat on the top.

6 Bake at 230°C/450°F/Gas Mark 8. The oven should be preheated to this temperature in order to ensure a successful result. For the rolls the setting should be increased to 240°C/475°F/Gas Mark 9.

VARIOUS SHAPES USING WHOLEMEAL DOUGH

From the basic Country Wholemeal dough hundreds of shapes can be made. Here are a few to try:

Coburg
Weigh the dough into 450g/1 lb rounds keeping the seam at the bottom. Grease a baking tray and place the dough on it. Cut the top in the following ways:

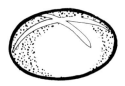

Traditional

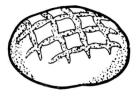

Crisscross

Straight cut

Tudor

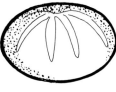

German

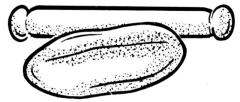

Slightly
flattened
(Greek style)

Cottage

This loaf epitomises the country baker and is a very
popular shape. Weigh the dough into two rounds.
The first should be 275g/10oz and the second
175g/6oz. Shape both into rounds and place the
smaller one on the top of the larger one. Press
down and insert your middle finger through the
centre right to the bottom. This seals both pieces
together. As a contrast cut the top around the
edges to give a rustic look to the baked loaf.

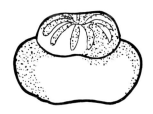

Rolls

All the above shapes can be transformed into rolls. Just weigh into 50g/2oz rounds and proceed as for the other loaves mentioned. You can make long, knotted or round baps. Round baps: Shape a 50g/2oz piece of dough until smooth on top, cover and rest for 10 minutes, then roll out flat like a pancake. Egg wash and dip in sesame seeds or dust with flour. Prove and bake at 230°C/450°F/Gas Mark 8 for 10-15 minutes. Crusty rolls should be baked for slightly longer (20-25 minutes). Remember that all these shapes freeze well so make larger batches than you actually require and store some for another time!

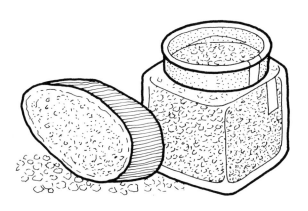

Harvest Festival

This is more for decorative purposes and requires a great deal of skill. If you wish to try then use the recipe for Country Wholemeal Bread but leave out the yeast as no aeration is required for this type of bread. Modelling with a dead dough is simple if you follow a pattern. The harvest festival wheatsheaf looks a complicated arrangement of modelled pieces of dough, but is quite straightforward.

| 1 | Pin out a piece of dough to this shape and dock the whole area with a fork to stop air pockets. |

| 2 | A rope of dough is then placed to form the stalks. |

| 3 | The ears are made using 25g/1oz pieces of dough rolled out long, then with a pair of scissors cut at various angles to create the ears of corn. Arranged neatly the overall effect is very realistic and will keep for months when baked. Egg wash twice and bake at 200°C/400°F/Gas Mark 6 for 40–60 minutes. |

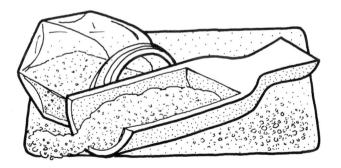

MORNING GLORY BREAD

Imagine rising in the early morning, the mist making way for the sun to shine, as you bite into a slice of delicious Morning Glory bread. What more could you ask? Here's the recipe.

Ingredients	Metric	Imperial	American
Liquid malt extract	25g	1oz	2 tbsp
Whole wheat grains	100g	4oz	1 cup
Warm water	450ml	16 fl oz	2½ cups
Whole meal flour	700g	1 lb 8oz	6 cups
Milk powder	25g	1oz	2 tbsp

Salt	1 tsp	1 tsp	1 tsp
Vegetable fat	25g	1oz	1 tsp
Honey	25g	1oz	2 tbsp
Yeast	25g	1oz	2 tbsp

1 Combine the malt extract, whole wheat grains and warm water. Leave overnight to soak. The grains will become soft and absorb the malty flavour.

2 Sieve the dry ingredients and add the malt mixture, fat and honey. Dissolve the yeast in a little warm water, add to the mixture and mix thoroughly for 5–10 minutes until smooth and elastic.

3 If using an ascorbic acid tablet to speed up fermentation just rest for 10 minutes before shaping. If using the traditional method of fermentation leave covered with oily polythene for 1 hour. Knock back and shape into the final loaf.

4 Grease tins and place dough, seam downwards, to prove for 40 minutes to 1 hour. Then bake at 220°C/425°F/Gas Mark 7.

HERB BREAD

If you like savouries, then this bread will evoke
summer evenings, the cool fragrance of thyme,
parsley, basil, oregano, marjoram and sage drifting
in through the windows. The aroma from this loaf
truly does fill the air! Use fresh herbs wherever
possible.
Note: If using fresh herbs, double the
measurements given here.

Ingredients	Metric	Imperial	American
Wholemeal flour	900g	2 lb	8 cups
Salt	1 tsp	1 tsp	1 tsp
Vegetable fat	50g	2 oz	4 tbsp
Yeast	40g	1½ oz	3 tbsp
Brown sugar	40g	1½ oz	3 tbsp
Warm water	575ml	1 pint 2 fl oz	2¾ cups
Thyme	½ tsp	½ tsp	½ tsp
Parsley	½ tsp	½ tsp	½ tsp
Basil	1 tsp	1 tsp	1 tsp
Oregano	½ tsp	½ tsp	½ tsp
Marjoram	½ tsp	½ tsp	½ tsp
Poppy seeds	1 tsp	1 tsp	1 tsp

1 Combine the flour and salt. Mix with the fat.

2 Mix the yeast and brown sugar in warm water and
add to the ingredients. Proceed to mix to a clear
dough and then add the herbs. Mix thoroughly.

3 Allow the dough to prove for 1 hour but knock
back after 45 minutes. Then you can weigh the
dough into various shapes. Prove on a baking
sheet or in tins for 45 minutes. Preheat the oven
to 230°C/450°F/Gas Mark 8. Decorate with poppy
seeds and bake for 30 minutes.

Suggested variations for Herb Bread

Baps: Weigh into 50g/2oz pieces. Shape into rounds, roll out flat and decorate with sesame seeds, oats or grated cheese (the cheese should be put on 5 minutes before removing from the oven.)

Pitta: Proceed as for Baps but roll out the rounds flat and leave plain. Bake in a very hot oven at 240°F/475°F/ Gas Mark 8 for 5–10 minutes. When baked open the centre and fill with your favourite fillings.

BAVARIAN RYE

A strong tasting bread, popular in Germany. There are many different varieties and this recipe produces a lighter loaf than some of the pumpernickels which are dark in colour and are an acquired taste. I have added carraway seeds to give a distinctive flavour.

Ingredients Sour dough	Metric	Imperial	American
Rye flour	300g	11 oz	3 cups
Yeast	8g	¼ oz	2 tsp
Warm water	300ml	½ pint	1½ cups
Wheatmeal	1 kg		
	175g	2 lb 10 oz	10½ cups
Rye flour	75g	3 oz	1 cup
Salt	25g	3-4 tsp	3-4 tsp
Yeast	40g	1½ oz	2 tbsp
Warm water	680ml	1 pint 4 fl oz	3 cups
Carraway seeds	15g	½ oz	1 tbsp

1. For sour dough place the rye flour, yeast and water into a mixing bowl and mix until clear. Cover and leave overnight in a warm place for the dough to mature.

2. Continue to mix all dry ingredients and add the sour dough. Dissolve the yeast in warm water and add to the mixture. Mix until clear and smooth. Add carraway seeds and mix for 1 minute. Leave to prove for 30 minutes. However, knock back after 20 minutes.

3 Weigh into a 450g/1 lb round or long shape and glaze with a flour and water mixture. This gives a nice finish to the crust. If you like carraway seeds, sprinkle some on top.

4 Grease tins or baking sheets and prove for 40 minutes before baking at 230°C/450°F/Gas Mark 8 for 30–40 minutes.

35

HARVEST CHEESE BREAD

A slice of wheatmeal bread but with the added taste of cheese and a hint of mustard and cayenne pepper is the ideal snack at lunchtime.

Ingredients	Metric	Imperial	American
Wheatmeal flour, 81%		1 lb	
extraction	800g	12 oz	7 cups
Salt	2 tsp	2 tsp	2 tsp
Milk powder	25g	1 oz	1 tbsp
Yeast	20g	¾ oz	¾ oz
Ascorbic acid tablet	½ tsp	½ tsp	½ tsp
Warm water	550ml	1 pint	
		4 fl oz	2½ cups
Cheddar cheese			
(grated)	225g	8oz	2 cups
Mustard	1 tsp	1 tsp	1 tsp
Cayenne pepper	½ tsp	½ tsp	½ tsp
Oats for topping			

1 Weigh the flour, salt and milk powder into a mixing bowl. The 81% extraction flour will be lighter when baked in both colour and texture.

2 Dissolve the yeast and ascorbic acid tablet in the warm water and add to the dry ingredients.

3 Proceed to knead the dough until smooth and clear (about 5–10 minutes, or 10–15 minutes by hand. Place in a polythene bag which has been oiled and leave for 45 minutes in a warm place.

4 Grate the cheese and mix with the mustard and cayenne pepper. After the dough has rested for 45 minutes in the bag add the grated cheese mixture and incorporate fully into the dough. Rest for 15 minutes and then weigh into 450g/1 lb or 900g/2 lb loaves. Shape into round cobs or roll out the smaller size into 2 long sausages. Join the ends together and twist the strands to form a plait. Place in greased tins, sprinkle oats on top and leave to prove for 15 minutes.

5 Bake at 230°C/450°F/Gas Mark 8 for 30 minutes. After 25 minutes baking time grate some cheese and sprinkle this on the top. Return to oven for 5 minutes or until golden brown.

Variations for Harvest Cheese Bread

Cheese and Onion Bread: Proceed as above but add 100g/4oz of onions to the cheese mixture. Sprinkle onion on the top instead of cheese.

Cheese and Tofu Bread: Repeat the procedure but add 100g/4oz of tofu to the cheese.

Cheese, Chives and Garlic Bread: Make and bake as above but add 2 heaped tablespoons of chives, and 2 finely. chopped garlic cloves to the cheese mixture.

Cheese and Curried Mixed Fruit: Instead of mustard and pepper, replace with curry powder, a little ginger and 100g/4oz of mixed dried fruits — sultanas, raisins, apples, etc.

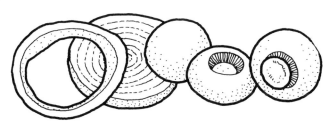

SAMOS BREAD

Sesame seeds impart a delicate flavour to bread. They are very nutritious and, if the seeds are roasted and added to the dough, they give a nutty taste to the bread when baked. Spread honey on slice — ideal for a teatime snack!

Ingredients	Metric	Imperial	American
Wholemeal flour	900g	2 lb	8 cups
Salt	2 tsp	2 tsp	2 tsp
Milk powder	25g	1 oz	2 tbsp
Roasted sunflower seeds	25g	1 oz	2 tbsp
Vegetable fat	25g	1 oz	2 tbsp
Yeast	1 tbsp	$\frac{3}{4}$ oz	1 tbsp
Honey	25g	1 oz	2 tbsp
Malt extract	25g	1 oz	2 tbsp
Warm water	575ml	1 pint 2 fl oz	$2\frac{3}{4}$ cups
Roasted sesame seeds	50g	2 oz	4 tbsp

1. Place all the dry ingredients except the seeds in a bowl and mix together thoroughly with the fat. Dissolve yeast, honey and malt extract into the warm water and add to the dry ingredients.

2. Using a dough hook begin by mixing on a slow speed for 5–10 minutes or until the dough is smooth. Then add the roasted seeds and mix for a further 5 minutes.

3. Weigh dough into 450g/1 lb portions making sure the seam is at the bottom. Grease a warm baking tin and prove the dough by placing in an oily polythene bag for 40 minutes, or until the dough rises just above the top of the lip of the tins.

4 Preheat the oven to 230°C/450°F/Gas Mark 8. Place the dough pieces in the oven and bake for 30 minutes until golden brown.

Suggested variation for Samos Bread

Kos Bread: If you prefer a different shape, make the dough into the shape of a football and then roll it flat like a pancake. Cut it into quarters and sprinkle sesame seeds on top or dust with flour. Prove on a greased baking sheet and bake the same as for Samos.

2. TEA TIME TREATS

COTTAGE TEA BREAD

Sweet tea breads — a change from biscuits — and more wholesome — makes wonderful bread and butter pudding, if there is any left over, that is!

Ingredients	Metric	Imperial	American
Wholemeal flour	900g	2 lb	8 cups
Milk powder	25g	1 oz	2 tbsp
Salt	1 tsp	1 tsp	1 tsp
Brown sugar	25g	1 oz	2 tbsp
Fresh yeast	40g	1½ oz	3 tbsp
Warm water	575ml	1 pint 4 fl oz	2¾ cups
Fresh egg	1	1	1
Vegetable margarine	25g	1 oz	2 tsp
Currants	275g	10 oz	2½ cups
Sultanas	225g	8 oz	2 cups
Raisins	175g	6 oz	1½ cups
Mixed peel	100g	4 oz	1 cup
Mixed spice	1 tsp	1 tsp	1 tsp

1   Mix together all the dry ingredients except the fruit and spice in a bowl. Add the yeast to the warm water and mix this in. Add the egg and fat until a smooth elastic dough is produced. Weigh the fruit and spice and add after the initial mixing has taken place. Combine thoroughly.

| 2 | Leave the mixture to prove in an oily polythene bag for 45 minutes in a warm place. Knock back and rest for 15 minutes. Weigh into 450°g/l lb rounds and shape as desired. The basic shape for this bread would be tins or round cob shapes, flattened and divided into 8. |

| 3 | Prove for 45 minutes and bake at 220°C/425°F/Gas Mark 7 for 25–30 minutes. After baking glaze the top with $\frac{1}{2}$ water mixture, with a little zest of lemon and spice. |

Variations for Cottage Tea Bread

HUNGARIAN STRESSEL WHIRLS

Ingredients	Metric	Imperial	American
Stressel Topping			
Wholemeal flour	175g	6oz	1½ cups
Vegetable margarine, melted	150g	5 oz	1½ cups
Brown sugar	175g	6 oz	1½ cups
Sesame seeds	50g	2oz	2 tbsp
Filling			
Brown sugar	75g	3oz	6 tbsp
Vegetable margarine	75g	3 oz	6 tbsp
Ground almonds	75g	3 oz	6 tbsp
Nutmeg	½ tsp	½ tsp	½ tsp
Prunes, destoned and chopped	50g	2 oz	4 tbsp

| 1 | Blend topping ingredients together to form a crumbly consistency. Refrigerate for 30 minutes before use. |

| 2 | For the filling cream the sugar and margarine and add the almonds and nutmeg to form a paste. |

| 3 | Take the dough for the Cottage Tea Bread (see above) and prove for 1 hour. Roll out to a rectangle. Spread the filling on top and sprinkle with the prunes. Roll up as for a Swiss roll, making sure the bottom has been egg washed to seal the ends. Cut into 2cm/1in squares and place on greased baking sheets, leaving room for expansion of each square. Egg wash and sprinkle Stressel mixture on top. Prove for 30 minutes. Bake at 220°C/425°F/Gas Mark 7. |

| 4 | After cooking leave to cool and enjoy with a cup of lemon tea! |

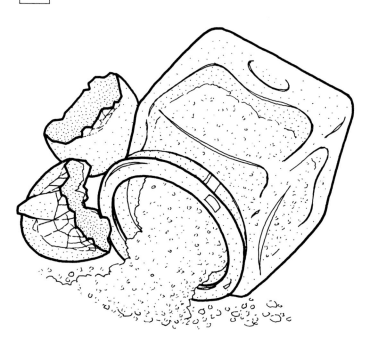

FREDA'S NUT BREAD

Nuts can be very tasty in bread. You can vary the type of nuts to suit yourself.

Ingredients	Metric	Imperial	American
Wholemeal flour	850g	1 lb 4 oz	7½ cups
Oats	100g	4 oz	1 cup
Salt	1 tsp	1 tsp	1 tsp
Soya flour	2 tsp	2 tsp	2 tsp
Brown sugar	40g	1½ oz	3 tbsp
Yeast	40g	1½ oz	1½ oz
Light malt extract	15g	½ oz	1 tbsp
Warm water	575ml	1 pint 2 fl oz	3 cups

Almonds, peanuts, cashews,			
hazelnuts, etc	225g	8 oz	2 cups
Currants	175g	6 oz	1½ cups
Dates	100g	4 oz	1 cup
Raisins	100g	4 oz	1 cup
Cinnamon	1 tsp	1 tsp	1 tsp
Vegetable fat	20g	¾ oz	1½ tbsp

1. Combine all the dry ingredients in a mixing bowl except the nuts fruit and spice. Mix the yeast and malt extract into warm water and add to the mixing bowl. Mix until smooth and clear.

2. Add the nuts, fruits, and spice and mix for a further 2 minutes until well integrated. Prove for 1 hour in an oiled polythene bag in a warm place.

3. Weigh the dough into 350g/12oz pieces and shape into rounds. Flatten into plate shapes, divide into 8 and egg wash the tops. Sprinkle nib nuts on top and place in a greased baking tin. Prove for 30–40 minutes and then bake at 230°C/450°F/Gas Mark 8.

4. After baking glaze with honey syrup mixture.

Variations
Nut Bread: Substitute the fruit for more nuts and add chopped brazils, walnuts and pecans as a change.
Apple and Sultana Bread: Add 225g/8oz apples instead of the nuts and 400g/14oz sultanas. Mix the apples with the cinnamon and proceed as for fruit and nut. When baked, glaze top with honey and sprinkle roasted wheatgerm on as well as a decoration.

FIGARO ROLLS

An unusual combination — honey and malted figs
— but well worth trying. Instead of making loaves
try these rolls; cut through the centre and toasted
with a little butter they are delicious at teatime.

Ingredients	Metric	Imperial	American
Wheatmeal flour	450g	1 lb	4 cups
Milk powder	20g	¾ oz	1 tbsp
Salt	1 tsp	1 tsp	1 tsp
Butter	40g	1½ oz	2 tbsp
Fresh yeast	25g	1 oz	1 oz
Warm water	275ml	½ pint	1¼ cups
Honey	75g	3 oz	6 tbsp
Figs, chopped	100g	4 oz	1 cup
Light malt extract	15g	½ oz	1 tbsp
Nutmeg	½ tsp	½ tsp	½ tsp
Zest of lemon or orange			
Sesame seeds	15g	½ oz	1 tbsp

1   Soak the figs together with the malt extract,
honey and nutmeg in some of the warm water for
1 hour, adding a little zest of orange or lemon.

2   Sieve the flour, milk powder and salt into a bowl
and blend in the butter. Dissolve the yeast in
warm water with a little honey.

3   Mix the dough thoroughly and add the fig
mixture. Mix for a further 5 minutes. Prove for 45
minutes in a warm place, knock back and rest for
15 minutes more. Weigh the dough into 50g/2oz
pieces and shape into rolls. Brush with egg wash
and dip the tops in sesame seeds.

4 Place the rolls on greased baking trays and prove for 30–45 minutes. Bake for 15 minutes at 230°C/450°F/Gas Mark 8. Cool and cut through the centre ready for spreading. These buns will freeze well if need be.

Variation:

Weigh the dough into a 450g/1 lb loaf, sprinkle bran on the top and glaze with honey. Instead of nutmeg you can use aniseed which imparts a delicate flavour, perfect on hot summer days.

PANASTAN BREAD

A trip to the forgotten land of Panastan and you'll
see the local baker there making this favourite fruit
bread. People there have been known to live over
100 years, but I don't know whether its the bread
that does it. It is delicious though!

Ingredients	Metric	Imperial	American
Sunflower seeds	15 g	½ oz	1 tbsp
Sesame seeds	15 g	½ oz	1 tbsp
Wheatgerm, roasted	25 g	1 oz	1 tbsp
Wheatmeal flour	450 g	1 lb	4 cups
Salt	1 tsp	1 tsp	1 tsp

Sultanas	175 g	6 oz	1½ cups
Mixed peel	25 g	1 oz	2 tbsp
Light malt extract	1 tsp	1 tsp	1 tsp
Honey	65 g	2½ oz	4 tbsp
Warm water	175 ml	¼ pint	¾ cup
Fresh yeast	25 g	1 oz	2 tbsp
Egg	1 large	1 large	1 large

1 Roast the sunflower seeds, sesame seeds and the wheatgerm until golden brown. Place all the dry ingredients in a bowl and blend in the margarine.

2 Dissolve malt extract and honey in the warm water with yeast and egg and mix until clear and smooth.

3 Mix the fruit, seeds and wheatgerm together and add to the dough. Combine thoroughly. Leave the dough to prove for 1 hour in an oily polythene bag in a warm place. Then weigh the dough into 2 x 450 g/1 lb loaves and the rest into 50 g/2 oz buns. Shape into long baton shape and place the seam at the bottom in a well greased baking tin. Prove for 40 minutes and bake at 230°C/450°F/Gas Mark 8.

Variations
Sprinkle wheatgerm on top before baking to give a wholesome texture to the finished loaf. Instead of wheatmeal use 100% wholemeal and sprinkle rolled oats or flaked wheatgrains on top before baking.

AUTUMN MIST CROWN

Chestnuts roasting on an open fire and ginger bringing a warm glow. These two things to make up this recipe, delicious during the autumn. Or try it all year round using Marron Glaće instead of freshly roasted chestnuts.

Ingredients	Metric	Imperial	American
Wholemeal flour	500 g	1 lb 2 oz	4 cups
Baking powder	20 g	¾ oz	1½ tbsp
Brown sugar	75 g	3 oz	6 tbsp
Salt	1 tsp	1 tsp	1 tsp
Mace	½ tsp	½ tsp	½ tsp
Vegetable fat	75 g	3 oz	6 tbsp
Egg whites	75 g	3 oz	6 tbsp
Milk	300 ml	½ pint	1 cup

Filling

Wholemeal cake crumbs, sieved	175 g	6 oz	1½ cups
Hazelnuts, ground	50 g	2 oz	4 tbsp
Brown sugar	50 g	2 oz	4 tbsp
Marron glace	100 g	4 oz	1 cup
Stem ginger, chopped	75 g	3 oz	⅓ cup
Rum or brandy	2 tbsp	2 tbsp	2 tbsp
Egg	1	1	1

1   Mix all dry ingredients together with the fat. Add the egg whites and milk. Mix for 3–5 minutes until the dough is soft and pliable.

2   For the filling, place the cake crumbs, hazelnuts, sugar, marron glaće, ginger and liquor together to form a soft paste using the egg to give the right consistency, suitable for spreading.

49

| 3 | Roll out the dough in a rectangle to make 2 crowns — approx 30 x 20 cm/12 x 8 in. Egg wash the dough and spread the filling all over it, leaving the bottom 2.5 cm/1 in free for sealing. Commence rolling from the top in Swiss roll fashion until it is completely rolled up. Join each end together in a circle and, using a pair of scissors, make little cuts around the top for decoration. Lay on a greased baking tray, egg wash and then rest the mixture for 10 minutes. |

| 4 | Bake at 230°C/450°F/Gas Mark 8 for 20–30 minutes. (This can be baked as 450 g/1 lb loaves at the same temperature.) When baked, glaze with honey, leave to cool and then slice to serve. |

Filling Variations
Replace stem ginger with sultanas, raisins or dates.
Replace rim with zest and juice of orange.

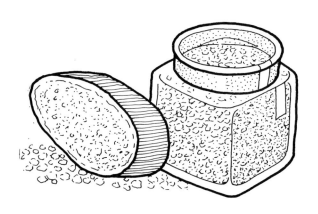

SPICY BUNS

One a penny — two a penny — hot cross buns. I'm afraid they will cost a little more today but they are well worth it with wholemeal flour.

Ingredients	Metric	Imperial	American
Wholemeal flour	450 g	1 lb	4 cups
Brown sugar	6 tbsp	6 tbsp	6 tbsp
Salt	½ tsp	½ tsp	½ tsp
Milk powder	25 g	1 oz	2 tbsp
Eggs	1	1	1
Vegetable margarine	75 g	3 oz	3 tbsp
Mixed spice	15 g	½ oz	1 tsp
Currants	150 g	5 oz	1 cup
Dates, chopped	25 g	1 oz	2 tbsp
Zest of lemon or orange			
Lemon peel	25 g	1 oz	2 tbsp
Yeast	60 g	1¾ oz	1¾ oz
Warm water	300 ml	½ pint	1¼ cups
'Cross' mixture			
Unbleached white flour	100 g	4 oz	1 cup
Vegetable oil	25 g	1 oz	1 tbsp
Baking powder	½ tsp	½ tsp	½ tsp
Water	100 ml	¼ pint	½ cup

1 For the buns mix all the dry ingredients together except the spice and fruit. Add the margarine and egg and blend.

2 Mix the spice with the dried fruit adding the zest and juice of the orange or lemon. Leave to soak until ready to use.

| 3 | Place the yeast in the warm water and add to the other ingredients. Mix to a smooth dough. Then add the soaked fruit and mix well until fully integrated. Leave for 1 hour to prove with a knock back after 45 minutes. Then shape into rounds. |

| 4 | To make the 'cross mixture' mix the dry ingredients together and add the oil and water until a soft paste is produced, suitable for piping through a small paper bag. Refrigerate until required. |

| 5 | Weigh the dough into 50 g/2 oz pieces and shape into rounds. Place on a greased baking trays and prove for 45 minutes further in a warm place. Make sure the buns are moist on top. Then, using the 'cross' mixture pipe crosses on top of the buns. Bake for 15 minutes at 230°C/450°F/Gas Mark 8. Glaze with the honey when baked. Don't wait to cool — tuck in right away! |

Variations on Spicy Buns

Using the basic fermented dough, a hundred varieties can be produced. Here are a few:

Whirley Curley: Roll out the dough to a rectangle, spread with vegetable oil and sprinkle brown or Demerara sugar over it. Roll up like a Swiss roll and cut into 1.5cm/¾ pieces. Lay these 1cm/½ in apart on greased baking sheets and prove for 40 minutes before baking at 230°C/450°F/Gas Mark 8 for 15 minutes. Glaze with honey and sprinkle tops with chopped walnuts.

London Buns: Take the plain dough and add 110 g/4 oz sultanas, 25 g/1 oz mixed peel, 25 g/1 oz chopped cherries, a little cinnamon and 1 egg. The whole is mixed thoroughly and cut into 50 g/2 oz pieces.

Place these on greased baking trays and prove for 40 minutes. Just before baking (as above) sprinkle Demerara sugar or chopped nuts on top.

Cinnamon, Apple and Sultana Flaps: Divide the unfruited dough into 50 g/2 oz pieces and shape into rounds. Roll out into oval shapes, egg wash the edges and place 1 tbsp cooked, chopped apple/sultana mixture in the centre of each one. Turn over and seal edges, egg wash and prove for 40 minutes. Either deep fry in hot oil or bake as above.

Cookie Swiss Buns: Using plain flour to make the dough, add in 100 g/4 oz carob chips and mix thoroughly. Roll out 50 g/2 oz pieces into long sausage shape buns. Prove and bake as above. When baked coat the tops in melted carob.

Bun Rounds and Loaves: Weigh the fermented dough in 350 g/12 oz pieces and shape into a round for buns, or into lengths for loaves. Roll out the bun round and divide into 8. Prove and bake as above for 20 minutes. Bake for 25–30 minutes if you are making the loaves. Honey glaze the tops when ready.

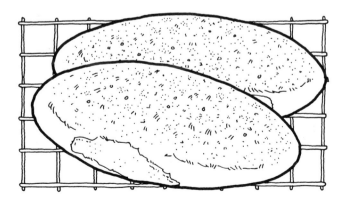

FRANZ'S ALMOND STOLLEN

Traditionally made at Christmas, the rich flavour of almonds is a treat at any time.

Ingredients	Metric	Imperial	American
Wheatmeal flour	500 g	1 lb 2 oz	4 cups
Rye flour	25 g	1 oz	2 tbsp
Brown sugar	50 g	2 oz	4 tbsp
Vegetable margarine	75 g	3 oz	6 tbsp
Fresh yeast	25 g	1 oz	2 tbsp
Warm water	300 ml	½ pint	1½ cups
Egg	1 medium	1 medium	1 medium
Currants	150 g	5 oz	1 cup
Sultanas	150 g	5 oz	1 cup
Cinnamon	½ tsp	½ tsp	½ tsp
Lemon peel	50 g	2 oz	4 tbsp
Zest and juice of orange or lemon			
Marzipan or almond paste	100 g	4 oz	4 oz

1 | Combine dry ingredients into a bowl. Add margarine and blend thoroughly. Dissolve yeast in warm water and add to the mixture. Add egg and knead for 10 minutes. The dough should be elastic when pulled.

2 | Mix the fruit with the cinnamon and orange/lemon zest and juice. Add this to the dough. Prove for 1 hour with a knock back after 45 minutes. Weigh the dough into 400 g/14 oz pieces. Roll out to an oval and egg wash the edges. Roll out the marzipan long, divide into 3 and place one into the centre of each of the

dough pieces or stollen. Fold the dough over like a turnover but not to the edge. Allow 2.5 cm/1in overlap. Prove for 40 minutes in a warm place and bake at 220°C/425°F/Gas Mark 7 for 25–30 minutes.

3 After removing from the oven glaze with honey icing. This is simply a little honey and margarine melted together. Sprinkle flaked roasted almonds on the top and eat when cold.

Variations
Instead of marzipan try a puree of dates and oranges. Or dried apricots and peaches pureed to a paste and added as a filling.

FOREST ROUNDS

Introducing carob to this recipe will give a unique flavour and hazelnuts will add a crunch. A little maple syrup spread on top will make these rounds a great start to the day!

Ingredients	Metric	Imperial	American
Wholemeal flour	450g	1 lb	4 cups
Baking powder	20g	¾ oz	1½ tbsp
Carob	40g	1½ oz	3 tbsp
Salt	1 tsp	1 tsp	1 tsp
Ground hazelnuts	50g	2 oz	4 tbsp
Crushed nuts, assorted	50g	2 oz	4 tbsp
Vegetable fat	75g	3 oz	6 tbsp
Honey	75g	3 oz	6 tbsp
Milk	300ml	11 fl oz	1⅓ cups
Vanilla essence	½ tsp	½ tsp	½ tsp

1   Place all the dry ingredients in a mixing bowl and blend together with the fat. Reserve some of the nuts for the topping.

2   Dissolve the honey in the milk and add to the dry mixture with the vanilla essence. Mix for 3–5 minutes until soft and pliable. Weigh into 350g/12oz pieces and shape into rounds. Then roll into flat scone shapes, divided into 6 portions, egg wash and sprinkle nuts on top.

3   Bake at 230°C/450°F/Gas Mark 8 on greased baking sheets for 15–20 minutes.

Variations

Roll out the dough and cut with a 7.5cm/3in cutter. Bake as individual rounds. Add carob chips to the recipe to give an American flavour. Roll out as for individual rounds and deep fry each 'scone' in vegetable oil for 3 minutes each side. Toss these in cinnamon flavour fine Demerara sugar, or coat tops in melted carob and dip in flaked hazelnuts.

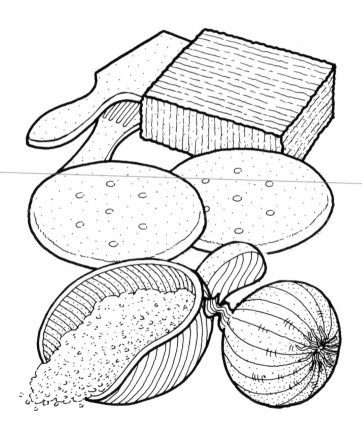

3. FANCY BREADS

TOLEDO BREAD

A passionate and spicy Mexican bread that warms the heart!

Ingredients	Metric	Imperial	American
Adzuki beans, cooked	50 g	2 oz	4 tbsp
Wholemeal flour	450 g	1 lb	4 cups
Salt	1 tsp	1 tsp	1 tsp
Soya flour	1 tsp	1 tsp	1 tsp
Vegetable margarine	20 g	1½ tbsp	1½ tbsp
Warm water	300 ml	½ pint	1¼ cup
Yeast	25 g	1 oz	1 oz
Canned tomatoes, chopped	50 g	4 tbsp	4 tbsp
Tomato puree	25 g	2 tbsp	2 tbsp
Ascorbic acid tablet (Vitamin C)	25 mg	25 mg	25 mg
Chilli powder	1 tsp	1 tsp	1 tsp
Oregano	½ tsp	½ tsp	½ tsp
Onion	25 g	1 oz	2 tbsp
Garlic clove, chopped	1	1	1

1 Soak adzuki beans overnight and cook for 40 minutes, making sure to bring to the boil. Always soak and well cook the beans before using in this recipe.

2 Combine the dry ingredients with the fat. Mix yeast with warm water and combine with dough. Add the tomatoes, tomato puree, ascorbic acid

tablet, chilli powder and oregano. Mix the dough thoroughly. Rest for 10 minutes.

3   Add the onion, beans and garlic and mix well. Again, rest for 10 minutes. Then weigh into 450 g/1 lb loaves and place into greased baking tins. The remainder can be made into batons or long torpedo rolls. Roll out and prove as for bread. For loaves bake at 230°C/450°F/Gas Mark 8 for 30 minutes. For rolls bake at the same temperature for 15 minutes. Just before removing from the oven sprinkle with cheese and bake for another 5 minutes.

Note: This goes well with chilli con carne or just on its own.

Variations

Pizza-type Roll: Roll out 450g/1 lb pieces of dough to a flat plate shape and oil the surface. Sprinkle with chopped mushrooms, peppers, onions, tomato sauce and cheese. Bake at 220°C/425°F/Gas Mark 7.

Method for plaiting 4 strand roll (J. H. Baps and Plaits)

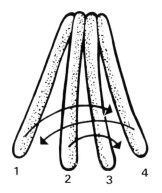

J. H. BAPS AND PLAITS

Named after John Harding, these incorporate a hint of aniseed, a touch of tomato in a light textured bap.

Ingredients	Metric	Imperial	American
Wheatmeal flour	450g	1 lb	4 cups
Cracked wheat	25g	1 oz	2 tbsp
Salt	½ tsp	½ tsp	½ tsp
Brown sugar	20g	¾ oz	1½ tsp
Vegetable margarine	25g	1 oz	2 tbsp
Fennel seeds	75g	3 oz	6 tbsp
Tomato puree	40g	1½ oz	3 tbsp
Fresh yeast	25g	1 oz	2 tbsp
Warm water	300ml	½ pint	1¼ cups
Sesame seeds	50g	2 oz	4 tbsp

1. Blend the dry ingredients together with the margarine, half the fennel seeds and the tomato puree. Dissolve the yeast in the warm water and add. Mix to a clear dough. Prove for 1 hour with a knock back after 30 minutes.

2. Weigh the dough into 50g/2 oz pieces and mould into rounds. Rest for 5 minutes. With a rolling pin roll out the dough into bap shapes, egg wash and dip half the batch into the fennel seeds and the other half into sesame seeds. Place on a greased baking tray and prove for 30 minutes. Bake at 230°C/450°F/Gas Mark 8 for 10 minutes or until golden brown. They should be soft to touch so do not over-bake.

Variations

Take 3 x 50g/2 oz pieces and roll out into long strips. Plait as for a 3 strand and sprinkle fennel or carraway seeds on. Prove for 40 minutes and then bake as above for 20–30 minutes.

CONIL'S SENSATIONAL BREAD

This loaf is guaranteed to keep you fit — if only for the time it takes to weigh out the ingredients!

Ingredients	Metric	Imperial	American
Wholemeal flour	900g	2 lb	8 cups
Oats	50g	2 oz	4 tbsp
Milk powder	25g	1 oz	2 tbsp
Cracked wheat	50g	2 oz	4 tbsp
Granary flour	100g	4 oz	1 cup
Salt	15g	½ oz	2 tsp
Vegetable margarine	100g	4 oz	1 cup
Honey	75g	3 oz	6 tbsp
Treacle	2 tsp	2 tsp	2 tsp
Warm water	475ml	1 pint	2 cups
Yeast	25g	1 oz	1 oz
Ascorbic acid tablet	25mg	25mg	25mg
Malt extract	2 tsp	2 tsp	2 tsp

The special ingredients

Sultanas	450g	1 lb	4 cups
Currants	225g	8 oz	2 cups
Raisins	100g	4 oz	1 cup
Dates	50g	2 oz	4 tbsp
Apricots, dried	50g	2 oz	4 tbsp
Apples, chopped	50g	2 oz	3 tbsp
Cherries, chopped	40g	1½ oz	3 tbsp
Mixed peel	25g	1 oz	2 tbsp
Citrion peel or figs	25g	1 oz	2 tbsp
Banana flakes, dried	25g	1 oz	2 tbsp
Desiccated coconut	25g	1 oz	2 tbsp
Ground almonds	25g	1 oz	2 tbsp
Ground hazelnuts	25g	1 oz	2 tbsp

Cashew nuts	25g	1 oz	2 tbsp
Peanuts, chopped	50g	2 oz	4 tbsp
Hazelnuts, chopped	50g	2 oz	4 tbsp
Walnuts, chopped	40g	1½ oz	3 tbsp
Almonds, chopped	40g	1½ oz	3 tbsp
Sunflower seeds, roasted	25g	1 oz	2 tbsp
Pumpkin seeds, roasted	15g	½ oz	1 tbsp
Sesame seeds, roasted	25g	1 oz	
Carraway seeds	½ tsp	½ tsp	½ tsp
Cinnamon	½ tsp	½ tsp	½ tsp
Mixed spice	½ tsp	½ tsp	½ tsp
Ginger	½ tsp	½ tsp	½ tsp

1 Place all the dry ingredients in a large mixing bowl and blend in the margarine. Dissolve honey and treacle in the water with the yeast, ascorbic acid tablet and the malt extract. Blend this with the other dry ingredients to make a dough. Mix until smooth and elastic and then rest for 5 minutes.

2 Measure all the special ingredients into another bowl and mix through by hand until well integrated. Combine these with the dough and mix. Rest for 5 minutes before weighing into 450 g/1 lb pieces. Place in greased tins and prove for 45 minutes. This dough will not rise as high as normal bread.

3 Bake at 220°C/42°F/Gas Mark 7 for 35–40 minutes. This loaf will mature whilst it is being kept and will freeze well.

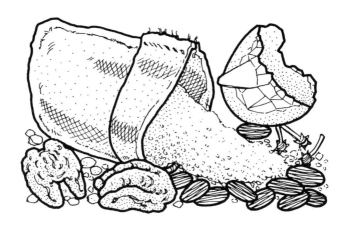

MALTED BANANA LOAF

A Jamaican surprise with a hint of malt. This loaf is very rich and similar in texture to cake rather than bread. Use fresh bananas to give that real flavour.

Ingredients	Metric	Imperial	American
Dark brown sugar	275g	10 oz	1¼ cups
Vegetable margarine	350g	12 oz	12 oz
Liquid malt extract	50g	2 oz	4 tbsp
Eggs	5 medium	5 medium	5 medium
Bananas	4	4	4
Apricots, dried	100g	4 oz	2 tbsp
Hazelnuts	100g	4 oz	2 tbsp
Wholemeal flour	450g	1 lb	4 cups
Baking powder	25g	1 oz	2 tbsp
Cinnamon	½ tsp	½ tsp	½ tsp
Rum	1 tsp	1 tsp	1 tsp

1. Cream the sugar and margarine together until light. Make sure the fat is soft before creaming. Dissolve the malt extract in the eggs which should be warm or at room temperature before using. Add in 3 stages beating every time.

2. Mash the peeled bananas and add to chopped apricots and chopped hazelnuts. Sieve the wholemeal flour, baking powder and cinnamon and add to the batter. Mix until clear. Add the bananas, apricots and hazelnuts plus the rum. Mix well.

3. Divide the mixture into 4 x 450g/1 lb pieces. Place each in a greased baking tin and sprinkle chopped hazelnuts on top. Bake at 180°C/350°F/Gas Mark 4 for 30–40 minutes.

SEVILLE BREAD

A refreshing tang gives this bread a certain
appeal . . . and one slice is never enough.

Ingredients	Metric	Imperial	American
Wheatmeal flour	550g	1 lb 4 oz	5 cups
Brown sugar	15g	½ oz	1 tbsp
Salt	½ tsp	½ tsp	½ tsp
Milk powder	15g	1 tbsp	1 tbsp
Vegetable shortening	15g	½ oz	1 tbsp
Yeast	25g	1 oz	1 oz
Warm water	350ml	12 fl oz	⅔ cup
Brown sugar	50g	2 oz	4 tbsp
Vegetable shortening	50g	2 oz	4 tbsp
Orange, zest and juice	1	1	1
Lemon, zest and juice	1	1	1
Lime, zest and juice	1	1	1
Sultanas	450g	1 lb	4 cups

1. Sieve all the dry dough ingredients and add the fat. Dissolve the yeast in the warm water and add to make a clear dough. Prove in a warm place for 1 hour covered to ensure it does not dry out. Then add the shortening into the dough.

2. Place the grated zest of the fruit and the juice in a bowl and mix with the sultanas. Add the fruit and sultanas to the dough. Rest for 5 minutes. Cream the sugar and shortening until light. Add this to the dough.

3. Weigh the dough into 450g/1 lb pieces, divide each piece into 3 long rolls and plait these strands together. Place on a greased baking tray and prove for 40 minutes. Bake at 220°C/425°F/ Gas Mark 7 for 30–35 minutes. Glaze when baked with honey.

NEVADA BREAD

1 Proceed as for Seville Bread but add the following
fruit at the last stage:

Apricots, chopped 75g/3 oz   Apples, chopped 225g/8 oz
Saffron ½ tsp in warm water   Dates, chopped 175g/6 oz

2 Weigh into 450g/1 lb pieces. Rest for 5 minutes
then roll out flat. Prove and bake as for Seville
Bread. When baked glaze with honey and sprinkle
with chopped walnuts.

WONG BREAD

A little oriental and very nutritious — this bread is made with bean sprouts and ginger. Try it with a slice of cheese on top and slipped under the grill.

Ingredients	Metric	Imperial	American
Wholemeal flour	450 g	1 lb	4 cups
Rye flour	275 g	10 oz	2½ cups
Soya flour	15 g	½ oz	½ oz
Salt	2 tsp	2 tsp	2 tsp
Vegetable margarine	15 g	½ oz	½ oz
Yeast	25 g	1 oz	2 tbsp
Warm water	500 ml	1 pint	2½ cups
Parmesan cheese	175 g	3 oz	⅓ cup
Onions, chopped	50 g	2 oz	4 tbsp
Garlic clove, chopped	1	1	1
Bean sprouts	225 g	8 oz	2 cups
Celery, chopped	2 sticks	2 sticks	2 sticks
Fresh ginger, finely chopped	15 g	1 oz	2 tbsp
A little vegetable oil			

1. Blend together wholemeal, rye and soya flours, salt and margarine. Dissolve the yeast in warm water and add to the dry ingredients. Mix to a clear dough and then add half the cheese. Prove for 1 hour in a warm place. Stir-fry the vegetables in a little oil. After 45 minutes add them to the dough and mix slowly until well combined in the dough. Rest for a further 15 minutes.

2 Weigh the dough into 450g/1 lb pieces. Roll out into rounds, mark into 8 portions and place on a baking tray. Prove for 40 minutes. Bake at 230°C/450°F/Gas Mark 8 for 30 minutes.

3 If you prefer, bake in a greased 450 g/1 lb baking tin and proceed as above. Eat within 2 days of baking or freeze until required. Makes 4 loaves.

TROPICANA BREAD

Coconuts and pineapple are the main ingredients in this Caribbean delight. Goes well with salads.

Ingredients	Metric	Imperial	American
Wheatmeal flour	850g	1 lb 4 oz	7½ cups
Rolled oats	100g	4 oz	1 cup
Sea salt	½ tsp	½ tsp	½ tsp
Soya flour	2 tsp	2 tsp	2 tsp
Brown sugar	40g	1½ oz	3 tbsp
Yeast	40g	1½ oz	1½ oz
Treacle	2 tsp	2 tsp	2 tsp
Warm water	625ml	1 pint	3 cups
Mixed nuts, chopped	100g	4 oz	1 cup
Mixed spice	½ tsp	½ tsp	½ tsp
Pineapple, chopped	175g	6 oz	1½ cups
Coconut flakes	50g	2 oz	½ cup
Ginger, ground	½ tsp	½ tsp	½ tsp
Desiccated coconut	100g	4 oz	1 cup

1   Place the dry ingredients into a bowl and add the margarine. Blend thoroughly. Dissolve the yeast and the treacle in the warm water and add to the other ingredients. Knead the dough until smooth. Prove for 45 minutes and then knock back. Add the nuts, spice, pineapple, coconut flakes, ginger and desiccated coconut. Reserve some coconut for topping. Mix well. Rest for 15 minutes.

2   Weigh into 5 x 1 lb/450g. Egg wash tops and dip in desiccated coconut. Bake at 230°C/450°F/Gas mark 8 for 25–30 minutes. Cool and eat within 2 days or freeze for future use.

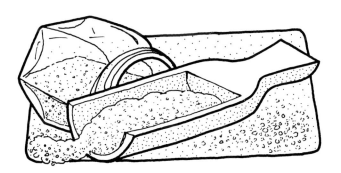

MANGO CURLS

This is good to accompany hot curry. The mangoes give a bitter sweet taste which is associated with India.

Ingredients	Metric	Imperial	American
Fresh mango	1	1	1
Ginger	1½ tsp	1½ tsp	1½ tsp
Raisins	350g	12 oz	3 cups
Wholemeal flour	450g	1 lb	4 cups
Salt	1 tsp	1 tsp	1 tsp
Vegetable margarine	40g	1½ oz	1½ oz
Milk powder	25g	1 oz	2 tbsp
Yeast	20g	¾ oz	¾ oz
Honey	25g	1 oz	2 tbsp
Warm water	300ml	½ pint	1¼ cups

1. Peel and core the mango. Chop into small cubes and add the ginger and raisins ready for later use.

2. Sieve flour and mix with salt, margarine and milk powder. Add yeast and honey to warm water and pour into the dry ingredients. Mix slowly for 5–10 minutes until dough is smooth and elastic. Prove for 1 hour, knocking back after 45 minutes. At this point add the mango mixture and mix through. Best for a further 15 minutes.

3. Weigh into 3 x 400g/14 oz pieces and shape into long batons or thick round loaves. Place on greased baking trays and egg wash. Prove for 40 minutes and bake at 220°C/425°F/Gas Mark 7 for 20 minutes until golden brown. When baked glaze with honey flavoured with ginger.

4. LOAVES, CAKES AND SCONES

WINTER VEGI LOAF

The cold dark evenings make us all hungry and what could be more nourishing than a loaf packed with fresh vegetables and pulses?

Ingredients	Metric	Imperial	American
Vegi Mix			
Dried lentils, peas, barley, rice or soup mix	100g	4 oz	1 cup
Turnip, diced	100g	4 oz	1 cup
Swede, diced	150g	5 oz	1½ cups
Leeks, chopped	75g	3 oz	6 tbsp
Onion, chopped	100g	4 oz	1 cup
Carrot, diced	100g	4 oz	1 cup
Parsley, freshly chopped	1 tsp	1 tsp	1 tsp
Garlic clove	1	1	1
Parmesan cheese	50g	2 oz	4 tbsp
Salt			
Pepper			
Wholemeal flour	675g	1 lb 8 oz	6 cups
Rye flour	225g	8 oz	2 cups
Rolled oats	100g	4 oz	1 cup
Salt	1 tsp	1 tsp	1 tsp
Milk powder	25g	1 oz	2 tbsp
Vegetable margarine	40g	1½ oz	1½ oz
Fresh yeast	25g	1 oz	1 oz
Warm water	550ml	1 pint	2½ cups
Liquid malt extract	2 tsp	2 tsp	2 tsp

73

<table>
<tbody>
<tr><td>1</td><td>Soak the dried pulses and cook until tender. Chop all the vegetables and place in a saucepan with a little oil. Saute for a few minutes until half cooked. Remove from heat and stir in the soup mix. The vegi mix is now ready. Leave to cool.</td></tr>
</tbody>
</table>

1 Soak the dried pulses and cook until tender. Chop all the vegetables and place in a saucepan with a little oil. Saute for a few minutes until half cooked. Remove from heat and stir in the soup mix. The vegi mix is now ready. Leave to cool.

2 Make the dough with the dry ingredients. Add the margarine and mix through. Dissolve the yeast in the water with the malt extract and add to other ingredients. Knead for 5–10 minutes. Prove for 1 hour, knocking back after 45 minutes. Then add the vegi mix. Continue mixing for about 1 minute further until well incorporated. Do not overmix; the vegetables should be seen as cubes when the loaf is cut.

3 Weigh the dough into 450g/1 lb pieces. Shape into long or round shapes depending on choice. Place on greased baking tray and prove for 40 minutes. Bake at 230°C/450°F/Gas Mark 8 for 30–35 minutes. Just before removing from the oven, sprinkle Parmesan on top. Bake until the grated cheese melts. Cool before eating.

KENTUCKY SWEET CORN BREAD

If you like sweet corn then this loaf is for you!
Again it uses no yeast so is quick and easy to make.

Ingredients	Metric	Imperial	American
Fine corn meal	450g	1 lb	4 cups
Wholemeal flour	225g	8 oz	2 cups
Baking powder	3 tsp	3 tsp	3 tsp
Salt	½ tsp	½ tsp	½ tsp
Honey	2 tsp	2 tsp	2 tsp
Egg	1 large	1 large	1 large
Vegetable oil	4 tbsp	4 tbsp	4 tbsp
Milk	425ml	¼ pint	1¾ cups
Sweet corn niblets	225g	8 oz	2 cups
Millet flakes	50g	2 oz	4 tbsp

 Blend all the dry ingredients together. Stir in the combined honey, egg, oil and milk. Mix well to form a soft dough. Add the sweet corn.

 Weigh the dough into 400g/14 oz pieces and shape into long batons. Place on a greased tray and egg wash. Sprinkle with millet flakes. Rest for 15 minutes. Bake at 220°C/425°F/Gas Mark 7 for 25–30 minutes.

Variations

Mould rounds from the dough and roll out 20 cm/8 in discs. Mark into 4 quarters and egg wash. Sprinkle with cornmeal and bake as for corn bread above.

Instead of sweet corn try some cooked split lentils and bake as for corn bread.

POTATO SCONES

Baked on a hot plate, these scones are ideal for winter tea time.

Ingredients	Metric	Imperial	American
Mashed potato	450g	1 lb	4 cups
Vegetable margarine	25g	1 oz	1 oz
Salt and pepper to taste			
Wheatmeal flour	65g	2½ oz	5 tbsp
Onion or cheese as desired			

1. Add the mashed potato to the margarine and season to taste. Sprinkle on the wheatmeal flour and blend in. Weigh the dough into 175g/6 oz pieces and shape round.

2. Dust the table with flour and roll out flat. Mark the dough into 4 quarters and cook on a hot plate for about 3 minutes for each sude. Serve immediately.

AZZIP PIE LOAF

Ingredients	Metric	Imperial	American
Filling			
Vegetable oil	1 tbsp	1 tbsp	1 tbsp
Onion, chopped	1 medium	1 medium	1 medium
Garlic clove	1	1	1
Tomatoes, canned	225g	8 oz	8 oz
Tomato purée	2 tbsp	2 tbsp	2 tbsp
Oregano	1 tsp	1 tsp	1 tsp
Basil	1 tsp	1 tsp	1 tsp
Salt	Pinch	Pinch	Pinch
Pepper	Pinch	Pinch	Pinch
Cornflour	1 tsp	1 tsp	1 tsp
Plain tofu or bean curd, chopped	225g	8 oz	8 oz
Cheddar cheese	175g	6 oz	1½ cups
Wholemeal flour	550g	1 lb 4 oz	5 cups
Salt	½ tsp	½ tsp	½ tsp
Bicarbonate of soda	1 tsp	1 tsp	1 tsp
Oregano	1 tsp	1 tsp	1 tsp
Vegetable margarine	40g	1½ oz	1½ oz
Liquid milk or buttermilk	300ml	½ pint	1¼ cups
Lemon juice	2 tsp	2 tsp	2 tsp

1. For the filling, place the oil, the onion and garlic clove into a saucepan and cook for 1 minute. Add the tomatoes and purée and continue to boil for 5–10 minutes. Add the herbs and seasonings. Stir in the cornflour to thicken the mixture and cook for 3 minutes on low heat. The filling is now ready. Add the chopped tofu and cool the whole mixture.

2. Place the dry dough ingredients in a mixing bowl and blend with the margarine. Add the milk and

lemon juice and mix slowly to form a soft dough.
Weigh the dough into 6 x 175g/6 oz pieces, make
into rounds and rest for 5 minutes. Roll out each
to a round disc 20 cm/8 in across. Egg wash the
edges of 3 discs and spread the filling equally
over them leaving a 1 cm/½ in margin around the
edges. Place on greased baking sheets and
sprinkle with cheese. Cover with another disc to
enclose the filling. Seal the edges.

3 Make a hole in the centre of each pie to allow
the air to escape. Egg wash and sprinkle with
either cheese or sesame seeds on top. (Add the
cheese towards the end of baking.) Bake at
230°C/450°F/Gas Mark 8 for 25–30 minutes.

79

COFFEE CAKES

A welcome treat after a vegetarian meal. Make them small as an alternative to petit fours.

Ingredients	Metric	Imperial	American
Wholemeal flour	450g	1 lb	4 cups
Baking powder	20g	¾ oz	4 tsp
Salt	1 tsp	1 tsp	1 tsp
Vegetable margarine	225g	8 oz	8 oz
Brown sugar	225g	8 oz	1 cup
Eggs	1 large	1 large	1 large
Currants	100g	4 oz	1 cup
Decaffeinated instant coffee	1 tsp	1 tsp	1 tsp

1. Sieve together the flour, baking powder and salt. Blend in the margarine and brown sugar and mix well. Add the egg and mix until a smooth clear dough is formed. It should be soft but not sticky. Add the currants and coffee in a little water. Knead well.

2. Weigh the dough into 40g/1½ oz pieces and shape into balls. Flatten with the palm of the hand. Place on greased baking trays allowing room to expand whilst they are baking. Press thumb into the centre of each cake and add a little honey. Bake at 220°C/425°F/Gas Mark 7 for 10–5 minutes or until golden and light.

3. When baked either leave plain or dip base in melted carob covering. In an airtight tin these cakes will keep for some time.

Variations

Instead of coffee use carob powder and a few chopped walnuts and dates.

Leave out the coffee and before baking make a dip in the centre of the biscuit to fill with raspberry conserve. Bake as before.

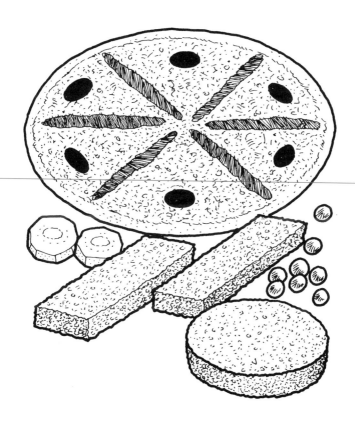

STILTON AND CELERY LOAF

A subtle flavour of Stilton amid the crunchiness of celery makes this a popular treat. This is a variation on the Azzip dough base.

Ingredients	Metric	Imperial	American
Wholemeal flour	550g	1 lb 4 oz	5 cups
Salt	½ tsp	½ tsp	½ tsp
Bicarbonate of soda	1 tsp	1 tsp	1 tsp
Liquid milk or buttermilk	300ml	½ pint	1¼ cups
Lemon juice	2 tsp	2 tsp	2 tsp
Vegetable margarine	40g	1½ oz	1½ oz
Stilton cheese	100g	4 oz	1 cup
Onion	1 large	1 large	1 large
Celery	3 sticks	3 sticks	3 sticks
Basil	1 tsp	1 tsp	1 tsp
Fresh parsley, chopped	2 tsp	2 tsp	2 tsp

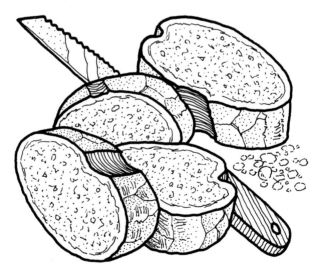

1   Proceed as for Azzip basic dough.

2   Add to the basic dough the grated or crumbled Stilton, the chopped onion, celery and herbs. Mix well.

3   Weigh the dough into 3 × 400g/14 oz pieces and shape into rounds. Roll these out to form discs 20 cm/8 in across and 1 cm/½ in thick. Place on a greased baking tray and divide into 8 portions. Egg wash and sprinkle with oats or sesame seeds. Bake at 230°C/450°F/Gas Mark 8 for 25 minutes.

SIZZY'S SHORTBREAD

Shortbread without butter would be like a Rolls without Royce! Try this recipe for size.

Ingredients	Metric	Imperial	American
Brown sugar	100g	4oz	½ cup
Honey	100g	4oz	½ cup
Butter	225g	8oz	1 cup
Vegetable shortening	225g	8oz	1 cup
Wholemeal flour	1½ lb	750g	6 cups

Blend the sugar, honey and fats to a paste. Blend in the flour and mix well until smooth. Keep cool. Roll out to about 5mm/¼in thickness and fork it all over to prevent bubbling. Divide into fingers but do not cut all the way through. Place on a greased baking tray and bake at 200°C/400°F/Gas Mark 6 until golden brown. Sprinkle with nibbed walnuts or Demerara sugar.

VIENNESE WHIRLS

A quick waltz and a Viennese whirl!

Ingredients	Metric	Imperial	American
Vegetable margarine	25g	1oz	2 tbsp
Wholemeal flour	225g	8oz	2 cups
Almonds, ground	50g	2oz	¼ cup
Soft brown sugar	100g	4oz	¼ cup

1 Cream the margarine and sugar together until light and fluffy. Blend with the flour and cream until light. Mix well until completely clear.

2 Pipe the mixture through a star nozzle bag on to a greased baking sheet allowing room for expansion. Bake for 10–15 minutes at 200°C/400°F/Gas Mark 6 until golden brown. When cool sandwich together with a little conserve or yoghurt.

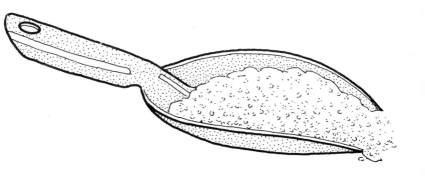

ONION CAKES

Ingredients	Metric	Imperial	American
Filling			
Vegetable margarine	25g	1 oz	2 tbsp
Wheatmeal flour	25g	1 oz	2 tbsp
Mustard	½ tsp	½ tsp	½ tsp
Milk	425ml	¾ pint	1¾ cups
Onions	2 large	2 large	2 large
Garlic cloves	2	2	2
Lemon juice	1 tsp	1 tsp	1 tsp
Grated cheese	100g	4 oz	½ cup
Parsley to garnish	1 tsp	1 tsp	1 tsp
Wholemeal flour	225g	8 oz	2 cups
Wheatmeal flour	225g	8 oz	2 cups
Sea salt	½ tsp	½ tsp	½ tsp
Milk powder	15g	½ oz	1 tbsp
Brown sugar	1 tsp	1 tsp	1 tsp
Mixed herbs	½ tsp	½ tsp	½ tsp
Pepper to season			
Ascorbic acid tablet	25mg	25mg	25mg
Fresh yeast	25g	1 oz	1 oz
Warm water	250ml	½ pint	1¼ cups
Egg	1	1	1
Vegetable oil	75g	3 oz	6 tbsp

1 To make the filling melt the margarine in a saucepan and add the wheatmeal flour and mustard. Stir until cooked. Pour the cold milk in slowly and whisk until there are no lumps left and a thick sauce results. Cook for 10–20 minutes and then add the partly cooked onions. garlic and lemon juice. Cook for a further 5 minutes and then cool. The sauce should be thick when cool.

2 Place all the dry dough ingredients in a bowl and add the oil, herbs and seasoning. Dissolve the yeast in the warm water and mix with the other

ingredients. Knead the dough to a smooth consistency. Rest for 10 minutes.

3 Weigh the dough into 75g/3 oz pieces pieces and shape into round rolls. Roll out each one to 15 cm/6 in across and 5 mm/¼ in thick. Oil the tops of each one and pour the filling into the centre.

4 Pour the filling into the centre of each of the dough discs making sure it does not overspill. Place on greased baking trays and sprinkle cheese on top. Prove for 30 minutes. Bake at 220°C/425°F/Gas Mark 7 for 20–30 minutes. Serve hot with a garnish of parsley.

Variations

Replace half the onion with chopped hard-boiled eggs and a little curry powder.

To any filling left over add 1 tin of tomatoes and a little tomato puree. Cook until thick and add a little oregano to give a delicious pizza filling.

Roll out the pizza dough as before, egg wash the edges and place a mixture of chopped vegetables in the centre. Bind together with mashed potato or bamboo shoots, peppers, tofu, sweet peas, rice or any combination of these. Serve hot with a vegetable sauce or cold with a salad.

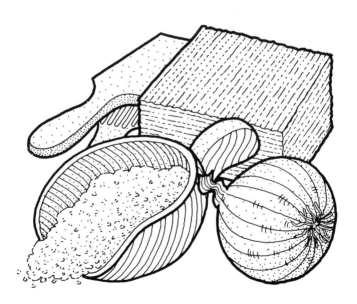

SAUERKRAUT BREAD

The slight piquancy of sauerkraut produces a taste which can be rather addictive in combination with carraway seeds!

Ingredients	Metric	Imperial	American
Sauerkraut	175g	6 oz	1½ cups
Carraway seeds	2 tsp	2 tsp	2 tsp
Dry mustard	1 tsp	1 tsp	1 tsp
Onion, chopped	1 small	1 small	1 small
Vegetable margarine	15g	½ oz	1 tbsp
Wholemeal flour	675g	1½ lb	6 cups
Rye flour	450g	1 lb	4 cups
Salt	1 tsp	1 tsp	1 tsp
Ascorbic acid tablet	25mg	25mg	25mg
Yeast	20g	¾ oz	¾ oz
Warm water	800ml	1½ pints	3½ cups
Honey	2 tsp	2 tsp	2 tsp

1 Combine the sauerkraut, carraway seeds, mustard and onion and leave ready for use.

2 Make dough with the margarine and the other dry ingredients by adding the yeast to the warm water and honey. The dough should be smooth. Rest for 10 minutes. Add the sauerkraut mixture and mix well into the dough. Rest for 5 minutes.

3 Weigh the dough in 450g/1 lb pieces and shape into rounds. Roll out slightly and make a hole in the centre. Place on greased baking trays and egg wash. Place the sauerkraut mixture in the central holes and prove for 40 minutes. Bake at 220°C/425°F/Gas Mark 7 for 30–35 minutes. This loaf is heavier than ordinary bread when baked.

SODA BREAD

An Irish tradition soda bread uses no yeast — the combination of buttermilk and soda gives all the lift required. A very quick alternative to yeast bread.

Ingredients	Metric	Imperial	American
Wholemeal flour	800g	1¾ lb	7 cups
Salt	1 tsp	1 tsp	1 tsp
Bicarbonate of soda	1 tsp	1 tsp	1 tsp
Vegetable margarine	40g	1½ oz	1½ oz
Buttermilk	625ml	1 pint	2¾ cups

1 Sieve the wholemeal flour, salt and bicarbonate of soda together and add the margarine, rubbing in until well integrated. Pour in the buttermilk and make a soft dough. Weigh into 3 x 450g/1 lb rounds. Roll out to round discs and mark into 4 quarters. Egg wash or dust over with wholemeal flour. Rest for 20–30 minutes before baking.

2 Bake at 230°C/450°F/Gas Mark 8 for 20–30 minutes or until the base sounds hollow when tapped.

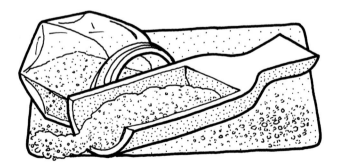

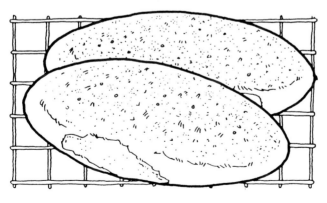

BARLEY SCONES

Barley meal or flour was once used for a lot of puddings and baked goods. You'll still find them on the health foods counter in larger stores.

Ingredients	Metric	Imperial	American
Barley flour	225g	8 oz	2 cups
Salt	Pinch	Pinch	Pinch
Bicarbonate of soda	½ tsp	½ tsp	½ tsp
Cream of tartar	½ tsp	½ tsp	½ tsp
Margarine	25g	1 oz	2 tbsp
Brown sugar	25g	1 oz	2 tbsp
Milk	100ml	4 fl oz	½ cup
Egg yolk for glazing			

1. Sift together flour, the salt, soda and cream of tartar. Rub in the fat, then mix in the sugar. Stir in the milk to make a soft dough.

2. Pat into a sheet 2cm (¾in) thick, and cut into round scones with a 5cm (2in) cutter. Heat the oven to 220°C/425°F/Gas Mark 7.

3. Lift the scones on to a greased, floured baking sheet, using a slice or broad spatula. Brush with egg yolk, and bake for 10–12 minutes.

4. Serve split and buttered with morning coffee.

DATE SLICES

These make a fibre-rich snack.

Ingredients	Metric	Imperial	American
Dates, stoned and chopped	225g	8 oz	2 cups
Honey	2 tbsp	2 tbsp	2 tbsp
Lemon juice	2 tbsp	2 tbsp	2 tbsp
Wholemeal flour	225g	8 oz	2 cups
Rolled oats	225g	8 oz	2 cups
Butter or margarine	225g	8 oz	I cup
Brown sugar	75g	3 oz	⅓ cup

1 Put dates, honey and lemon juice in a pan and cook gently until dates are soft. Allow to cool slightly.

2 Mix flour and oats, rub in butter or margarine, and stir in sugar. Press half this mixture into a shallow 20 cm (8in) square tin, greased and lined. Spread date mixture evenly over this, and then cover with the remaining flour and oat mixture. Press down firmly.

3 Cook for 35 minutes at 190°C/375°F/Gas Mark 5. Cut into slices while warm, and remove from tin when cold.

WHOLEMEAL SCONES

A traditional favourite at tea time. Instead of dairy cream try home-made yoghurt sandwiched with a fresh fruit preserve.

Ingredients	Metric	Imperial	American
Wholemeal flour	450g	1 lb	4 cups
Baking powder	20g	¾ oz	4 tsp
Brown sugar	75g	3 oz	6 tbsp
Salt	1 tsp	1 tsp	½ tsp
Vegetable oil	75g	3 oz	6 tbsp
Milk	300ml	½ pint	1¼ cups

| 1 | Sieve together the dry ingredients and mix in the oil. Add the milk in stages and mix until a soft dough results. Mix thoroughly. Weigh into 225g/8 oz pieces and shape into rounds. Roll out to 2 cm/1 in thickness and 15 cm/16 in across. Mark into 4 quarters and egg wash. Rest for 15–20 minutes before baking. |

| 2 | Bake at 230°C/450°F/Gas Mark 8. Do not overbake scones but leave them for 15–20 minutes. |

Variations

Add 75g/3 oz mixed dried fruit or nuts. Make sure the nuts are chopped first and roasted before adding to the dough.

For individual scones, roll out the dough to 2 cm/1 in and using a 7 cm/3 in cutter cut out scones. Egg wash, rest and bake as above for 10–15 minutes.

Instead of baking try deep frying at 180°C/360°F for 3 minutes each side. Toss in fine brown sugar or roasted ground nuts.

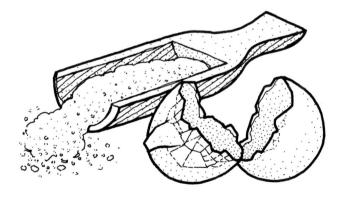

HONEY AND ALMOND CAKE

Ingredients	Metric	Imperial	American
Carrots, grated	250g	9 oz	2 cups
Almonds, chopped	65g	2½ oz	¼ cup
Eggs	2	2	2
Honey, warm	100ml	4 fl oz	¼ cup
Corn oil	4 tbsp	4 tbsp	4 tbsp
Milk	150ml	¼ pint	½ cup
Wholemeal flour	125g	5 oz	¼ cup
Salt	½ tbsp	½ tbsp	½ tbsp
Bicarbonate of soda	½ tbsp	½ tbsp	½ tbsp
Cinnamon, ground	2 tbsp	2 tbsp	2 tbsp
Lemon glacé icing			

1. Grease a 220mm (8 or 8½in) square cake tin.

2. Mix together the grated carrots and nuts. Beat the eggs in a mixing bowl, gradually adding the honey, oil and milk. Mix in the carrots and nuts.

3. Sift together the flour, salt, soda and cinnamon, and stir them into the carrot mixture.

4. Spread the batter evenly in the tin, and bake for 1-1¼ hours at 150°C/300°F/Gas Mark 2.

5. Cool in the tin for 10 minutes, then finish cooling on a wire rack. Ice when cold.

HIGH GRAIN PASTRY

This short, crisp pastry can be used as a base for hundreds of pies, flans and cakes.

Ingredients	Metric	Imperial	American
Vegetable margarine	225g	8oz	1 cup
Soft brown sugar	100g	4oz	¼ cup
Egg, large	1	1	1
Bran	50g	2oz	⅓ cup
Wholemeal flour	375g	12oz	3 cups

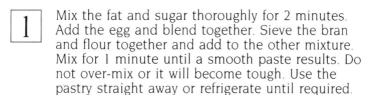

1   Mix the fat and sugar thoroughly for 2 minutes. Add the egg and blend together. Sieve the bran and flour together and add to the other mixture. Mix for 1 minute until a smooth paste results. Do not over-mix or it will become tough. Use the pastry straight away or refrigerate until required.

GRANVILLE CAKES

Many years ago the Cornish tin miners used to take these delicious cakes with them whilst they were working underground. A Cornish pasty and a Granville cake for lunch!

Ingredients	Metric	Imperial	American
Wholemeal flour	450g	1 lb	4 cups
Baking powder	20g	¾ oz	4 tsp
Salt	½ tsp	½ tsp	½ tsp
Vegetable margarine	100g	4 oz	4 oz
Brown sugar	100g	4 oz	½ cup
Egg	1	1	1
Milk	300ml	½ pint	1¼ cups
Vanilla essence	½ tsp	½ tsp	½ tsp
Currants	50g	2 oz	¼ cup
Sultanas	50g	2 oz	¼ cup
Cinnamon	½ tsp	½ tsp	½ tsp
Zest of orange and lemon	1 each	1 each	1 each

1 Sieve together the flour, baking powder, salt and then add the margarine and sugar. Mix to a fine crumble. Add the egg, milk and vanilla essence and mix to a soft sticky dough.

2 Mix all the dried fruits with the cinnamon and zest and add to the dough. Mix well.

3 Deposit 2 tbsp of the mixture on to greased baking trays. Use a spoon and leave looking rough on top. Allow room to expand when baked. Egg wash and sprinkle chopped almonds on top. Bake at 220°C/425°F/Gas Mark 7 for 15 minutes until lightly baked.

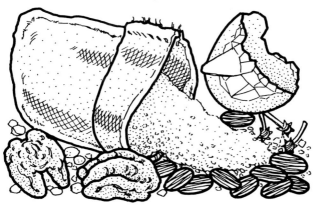

99

BRIOCHE

In French bakeries you can see brioche in all shapes
and sizes. It is a bread rich in eggs and butter, so
be careful. Replace the butter if you wish with
margarine. The bread is so light you won't notice
the calories.

Ingredients	Metric	Imperial	American
Fresh yeast	40g	1½ oz	1½ oz
Milk and water mixed			
half and half	175ml	¼ pint	¾ cup
Wheatmeal flour	225g	8 oz	2 cups
Wholemeal flour	675g	1 lb 8 oz	6 cups
Honey	40g	1½ oz	3 tbsp
Eggs	8	8	8
Salt	½ tsp	½ tsp	½ tsp
Butter or vegetable			
margarine	400g	14 oz	1¾ cups

1 Add the yeast, milk/water to the wheatmeal flour
to make a dough. Leave for 30 minutes to
ferment. To this dough add the wholemeal flour,
honey eggs and salt and knead well. Melt the
butter or margarine and pour on to the dough.
Continue mixing until dough is clear and well
kneaded. Prove for 1 hour in a warm place — or
better still 6 hours in a cool place. This will
improve texture of the finished loaf.

2 Weigh the dough into 400g/14 oz pieces or 25g/ 1 oz pieces for individual rolls and buns. Grease a fluted Brioche tin or Kougloff tin and and mould dough round. Place into tin and prove for 40 minutes. Bake at 200°C/425°F/Gas Mark 7 for 30 minutes or, for the smaller rolls, 230°C/450°F/Gas Mark 8 for 10–15 minutes. The smaller brioche are baked in small flutted patty tins.

Variations

Spicy Apple Brioche

Proceed as for the individual brioche. Roll out and fill the centre with a mixture of cooked apple, wholemeal breadcrumbs, sultanas and cinnamon. Turnover the dough and cover the filling completely. Place into greased fluted patty tins and prove. Bake as for plain brioche.

Nut Tofu Brioche

Make a filling paste from: 100g/4 oz tofu, 50g/2 oz cashew nuts roasted and chopped, 50g/2 oz mixed chopped vegetables, 25g/ 1 oz onion chopped, 1 clove of garlic, 1 tsp of mixed herbs, salt and pepper, and ½ tsp of mustard. Fill the dough as for the apple recipe above. Prove and bake as before.

OLD JOE'S MALT BREAD

I remember tasting this loaf when I was a mere lad
and always being told 'it will keep you young and
healthy'. Well I'm healthy, but not so young now.
Try it — it may work for you!

Ingredients	Metric	Imperial	American
Wholemeal flour	900g	2 lb	8 cups
Salt	2 tsp	2 tsp	2 tsp
Vegetable margarine	15g	½ oz	½ oz
Yeast	25g	1 oz	1 oz
Cool water	550ml	1 pint	2½ cups
Honey	3 tbsp	3 tbsp	3 tbsp
Treacle	2 tbsp	2 tbsp	2 tbsp
Liquid malt extract	60g	2½ oz	⅓ cup
Sultanas	350g	12 oz	3 cups
Dates, chopped	100g	4 oz	1 cup

1   Place the dry ingredients into a mixing bowl and
add the margarine. Stir well. Dissolve the yeast in
cool water and add the honey, treacle and malt
extract. Pour this mixture into the dry ingredients.
Mix dough for 10 minutes until smooth and clear.
Add the dried fruits and mix well in.

2   Prove the dough in an oiled polythene bag for
1½ hours, knocking back after 1 hour. Weigh the
dough into 4 x 450g/1 lb pieces and shape into
long batons. Place into greased tins and prove for
45 minutes. Then bake at 180°C/350–F/Gas
Mark 4 for 35–40 minutes. Make sure the loaf
doesn't get too dark.

3   When baked glaze with honey syrup. The loaf will
keep for several days.

CUSTARD FILLING

Ingredients	Metric	Imperial	American
Milk	225ml	½ pint	1 cup
Vanilla essence	Few drops	Few drops	Few drops
Eggs	1	1	1
Honey	25g	1 oz	2 tbsp
Cornflour	50g	2 oz	4 tbsp

Bring the milk to the boil with the vanilla essence. Whisk the eggs, honey and cornflour and add gradually to the milk. Whisk continuously until it thickens. Cook for a further 3–5 minutes until very thick. Leave to cool and cover to avoid skinning.

VARIETIES

Danish Whirls
Roll out Danish pastry to 5 mm/½ in thickness. Spread Franzipan filling thinly over the surface and fold in half. Cut into narrow strips 20 cm/8 in long and twist them 4 or 5 times. Place on greased baking trays, egg wash and sprinkle with chopped almonds. Prove for 30 minutes and then bake at 220°C/425°F/Gas Mark 7 for 10–15 minutes. When baked glaze with low sugar apricot purée. Finish with a cherry on top.

Croissant Crescent
Roll out the pastry to 5 mm/½ in thickness and cut into strips 10 cm/4 in wide. Then cut into triangles along the length of the strips. Egg wash and pipe a

little franzipan or almond paste on to the top of each. Roll up each Swiss roll fashion and keep the point on top. Egg wash, prove and bake at 220°C/425°F/Gas Mark 7 for 15 minutes. For croissants leave plain, egg wash, prove and bake as before.

Belgian Danish

Roll out pastry, egg wash and spread franzipan or custard over the surface. Sprinkle a little cinnamon on the custard with a few sultanas or sprinkle currants on the franzipan with a pinch of nutmeg. Begin rolling like a Swiss roll. Cut 1 cm/½ in thick pieces and place flat on greased baking trays, allowing room for expansion. Prove and bake at 220°C/425°F/Gas Mark 7 for 10–15 minutes. When baked glaze with apricot purée and sprinkle with flaked almonds.

Fruit Turnovers

Roll out the pastry to 3mm thick and cut into 10 cm/4 in squares. In the centre of each square place the filling of your choice (apples, sultanas, etc.) and taking one corner fold it diagonally to cover the filling. Egg wash, prove and bake as above for 15–20 minutes. Glaze with honey or apricot purée. Sprinkle sesame seeds or nuts on the top.

Danish Fruit Pastry

Roll out the pastry to 7 cm/3 in strips about 30 cm/ 12 in long. Egg wash and pipe a little lemon curd or strawberry preserve along the centre. On top of this pipe a line of franzipan filling and sprinkle either coconut or any other dried fruit on the franzipan. Cover with another strip which you can decorate with knife cuts. Place on a baking tray, egg wash, prove, glaze and sprinkle with nibbed almonds. Cut into 4 cm/1½ in slices. Bake as before and serve with almond flavour yoghurt.

DANISH PASTRIES

An endless variety can be made from just the basic pastry savoury as well as sweet. Very similar to flaky pastry but enriched with egg and yeast to produce a mellow eating treat.

Ingredients	Metric	Imperial	American
Wheatmeal flour	225g	8 oz	2 cups
Wholemeal flour	225g	8 oz	2 cups
Vegetable margarine	25g	1 oz	1 oz
Milk powder	25g	1 oz	1 oz
Brown sugar	25g	1 oz	1 oz
Salt	½ tsp	½ tsp	½ tsp
Fresh yeast	20g	¾ oz	¾ oz
Cold water	200ml	¼ pint	¾ cup
Egg	1 large	1 large	1 large
Butter	225g	8 oz	8 oz

1. Sieve the flour and rub in the margarine. Add the milk powder, sugar and salt and mix through. Crumble the yeast in some of the cold water and add the egg. Add to other ingredients to form a smooth dough. The water needed may vary so add gradually. Rest for 30 minutes and cover with a damp cloth to stop the dough skinning.

2. Roll out the dough to a rectangle. Dust any surplus flour from the surface. Add the butter by dabbing small pieces over the dough. Fold it in. Roll out the dough to 1 cm/½ in thickness and repeat, rest and repeat, rest and repeat. Then rest for 30 minutes. The pastry is now ready to work into shapes. Keep refrigerated or freeze if not required immediately.

Hints On Making Danish Pastry

1 Do not leave the pastry out of refrigeration when not being used.

1 Refrigerate pastry when not required or it will rise and be useless.

2 Prove in a dry atmosphere.

3 Wholemeal pastry has a tendency to absorb more water. Allowance should be made for this.

4 Wholemeal pastries are darker in colour so be careful when baking.

Here are a few fillings for Danish Pastry and also a few varieties of the original for the pastry itself.

SAVOURY DANISH PASTRY

Proceed as for sweet Danish Pastry but omit the sugar. This pastry is ideal for sausage rolls, cheese rolls and as a base for pies and quiches. Here is an ideal filling to go with it.

Noodle Strudel

Ingredients	Metric	Imperial	American
Tagliatelle	50g	2 oz	4 tbsp
Brown rice, dried	50g	2 oz	4 tbsp
Onion, chopped	75g	3 oz	6 tbsp
Carrots	50g	2 oz	4 tbsp
Celery	50g	2 oz	4 tbsp
Mushrooms	25g	1 oz	2 tbsp
Green pepper	25g	1 oz	2 tbsp
Red pepper	25g	1 oz	2 tbsp
Bean sprouts	50g	2 oz	4 tbsp
Tofu	50g	2 oz	4 tbsp
Soya sauce	Few drops	Few drops	Few drops
Vegetable oil	2 tbsp	2 tbsp	2 tbsp
Garlic cloves	2	2	2

1 Boil the noodles or tagliatelle and brown rice separately in boiling salted water until cooked. Stir fry the vegetables and tofu in a little oil, add the soya sauce and mix with the noodles and rice. Cool before use.

2 Roll out the Savoury Danish Pastry into 2 x 10 cm/4 in long strips to suit the baking tray you are using. Egg wash and put the noodle filling down the centre. Seal it with the other strip and egg

wash. Sprinkle the top with sesame seeds. Prove and then bake at 220°C/425°F/Gas Mark 7 for 25–30 minutes. Cut into slices and serve hot or cold.

Variations

Cut pastry into 10 cm/4 in squares, egg wash and put a little filling in the centre. Enclose corners to centre covering the filling. Egg wash, prove and bake at 220°C/400°F/Gas Mark 6 for 15–20 minutes.

JEAN'S TOFU AND APPLE FLAN

A fruit flan with a difference. The pastry is made with yeast. One slice with a little yoghurt completes any vegetarian meal.

Ingredients	Metric	Imperial	American
Pastry			
Wholemeal flour	175g	6 oz	1½ cups
Milk powder	25g	1 oz	2 tbsp
Brown sugar	25g	1 oz	2 tbsp
Vegetable margarine	25g	1 oz	2 tbsp
Fresh yeast	8g	¼ oz	¼ oz
Cold water	2 tbsp	2 tbsp	2 tbsp
Egg	1	1	1
Salt	Pinch	Pinch	Pinch
Tofu Filling			
Water	100ml	¼ pint	½ cup
Cornflour	25g	1 oz	2 tbsp
Tofu	175g	6 oz	1½ cups
Vegetable oil	50g	2 oz	¼ cup
Vanilla essence	Few drops	Few drops	Few drops
Zest of lemon	1	1	1
Apples	1 kg	1½ lb	1½ lb
Walnuts	50g	2 oz	4 tbsp
Cinnamon	½ tsp	½ tsp	½ tsp
Honey Glaze			
Gelatine	2 tbsp	2 tbsp	2 tbsp
Water	150ml	¼ cup	½ pint
Honey	25g	1 oz	2 tbsp

1 Filling: Boil the water and add the cornflour. Cook until thickened. Add the tofu and oil plus the vanilla essence and the lemon zest. Cool

2 Pastry Base: Sieve the flour and add milk powder, sugar, margarine and blend together. Dissolve the yeast in the water and add the egg and salt. Mix to a smooth dough and rest for 10 minutes. Then line 2 x 20 cm/8 in flan cases with the dough.

3 Spoon the filling into the base but only ¼ full at this stage. Cook the apples with a little cinnamon and pour into the flan as well. Cut the remaining apples into slices and arrange in a spiral pattern to cover the apple purée beneath.

111

| 4 | Rest for 10–20 minutes before baking at 200°C/400°F/Gas Mark for 30–40 minutes or until the apple is slightly crisp around the edges. |

| 5 | Glaze: Dissolve the gelatine in the water and heat to a clear state. Add the honey and glaze the flan with this mixture when it is cool. Sprinkle with nibbed walnuts and chill before serving. |

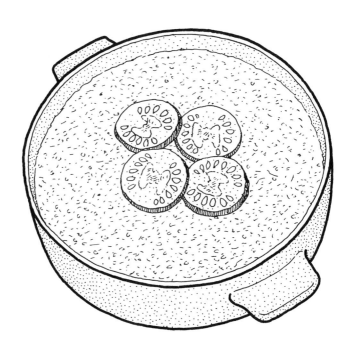

FRANZIPAN FILLING

Ingredients	Metric	Imperial	American
Vegetable margarine	225g	8 oz	1 cup
Brown sugar	225g	8 oz	1 cup
Eggs, warmed	4	4	4
Wholemeal cake			
crumbs	100g	4 oz	1 cup
Almonds, ground	100g	4 oz	1 cup
Rice, ground	25g	1 oz	2 tbsp
Wholemeal flour	25g	1 oz	2 tbsp
Almond essence	Few	Few	Few
	drops	drops	drops

 Cream the margarine and sugar to a light consistency. Add the eggs and beat until light. Sieve the dry ingredients and add to the mixture. Mix well until clear. Flavour with almond essence.

SEBASTIAN'S SAVOURY TARTS

With the added protein of tofu this is an ideal snack.

Ingredients	Metric	Imperial	American
Pastry base			
Wheatmeal flour	225g	8 oz	2 cups
Wholemeal flour	225g	8 oz	2 cups
Vegetable margarine	25g	1 oz	1 oz
Milk powder	25g	1 oz	2 tbsp
Salt	½ tsp	½ tsp	½ tsp
Fresh yeast	20g	¾ oz	¾ oz
Cold water	200ml	¼ pint	¾ cup
Egg	1	1	1
Butter	225g	8 oz	8 oz
Tofu Filling			
Tofu	225g	8 oz	8 oz
Vegetable oil	100g	4 oz	8 tbsp
Tomato purée	50g	2 oz	4 tbsp
Salt and pepper to taste			
Vegetable Filling			
Carrots, chopped	2	2	2
Onion, chopped	1	1	1
Celery stalk, chopped	1	1	1
Leek, chopped	1	1	1
Potato, cubed	1	1	1
Peas	100g	4 oz	1 cup
Garlic clove, chopped	1	1	1
Mixed herbs	½ tsp	½ tsp	½ tsp

| 1 | Make the dough by sieving the flour and adding the margarine. Add the milk powder and salt and mix through. Crumble the yeast in the cold water and add the egg. Add to the other ingredients to form a smooth dough. The water may vary according to needs so add gradually. Add the butter. Rest for 30 minutes. |

| 2 | Place the tofu in a blender with oil and tomato purée. Season and blend until smooth. |

| 3 | Prepare and boil the vegetables until cooked. Blanch the garlic and add with the herbs. |

115

4	Line 10 individual flan cases with the pastry dough and bake blind at 200°C/400°F/Gas Mark 6 for 15 minutes, filling each with dried beans to prevent them from blowing in the centre. When baked and cool add a little tofu filling to the base and cover with the mixed vegetables. Glaze with a sweet and sour sauce or a soya cornflour sauce. Serve with a sprig of parsley in the centre either hot or cold.

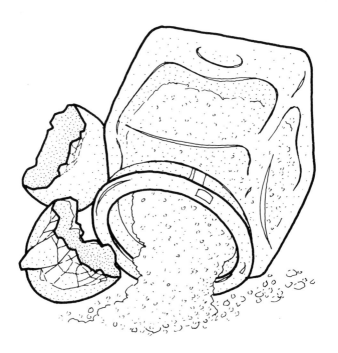

SALMON CHEESECAKE

A quick, simple refreshing stater to any meal. Serves 10.

Ingredients	Metric	Imperial	American
Vegetable margarine	75g	3 oz	3 oz
Wholemeal biscuits, crushed	150g	5 oz	1¼ cups
Rolled oats, roasted	25g	1 oz	2 tbsp
Filling			
Low fat curd cheese	100g	4 oz	4 oz
Tofu	100g	4 oz	4 oz
Vegetable oil	50g	2 oz	4 tbsp
Lemon juice	1 tbsp	1 tbsp	1 tbsp
Natural yoghurt	150g	5 oz	¼ pint
Eggs, separated	3	3	3
Gelatine	15g	½ oz	1 tbsp
Pink salmon, drained	1 tin	1 tin	1 tin

Salt and pepper to taste

Garnish

Cucumber slices, lemon slices and watercress.

1 Melt the margarine and mix in the crushed biscuits and oats. Press into a 23 cm/9 in flan ring, with a loose bottom if possible.

2 Beat together the cheese, tofu, oil, lemon juice, yoghurt, egg yolks and salmon. Stir in the dissolved gelatine. Whisk the egg whites to a peak and fold into the mixture. Season. Pour into the flan cases and chill until firm. When set remove from case and decorate with cucumber and lemon slices. Garnish with watercress.

Variations
Instead of salmon try tuna or sardines.

As an alternative to fish fresh summer vegetables, e.g. courgettes, sliced French beans, etc.

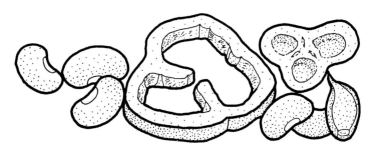

TOFU QUICK QUICHE

Ingredients	Metric	Imperial	American
Onion, chopped	1	1	1
Garlic clove	1	1	1
Mushrooms	50g	2 oz	2 oz
Soya sauce	Few drops	Few drops	Few drops
Vegetable oil	1 tbsp	1 tbsp	1 tbsp
Tofu, mashed	225g	8 oz	8 oz
Grated cheese	75g	3 oz	6 tbsp
Water	150ml	¼ pint	½ cup
Carrot, grated	1	1	1
Sesame seeds	25g	1 oz	2 tbsp

|1| Line a 20 cm/8 in flan case with yeast pastry.

|2| Chop onion, garlic, mushrooms and soya sauce and place in the same pan. With a little oil just sweat the vegetables and then transfer to pastry case.

|3| Blend together the tofu, cheese and water and pour over the vegetables covering them completely. Grate the carrot on top and sprinkle with sesame seeds. Rest for 10 minutes. Bake at 220°C/400°F/Gas Mark 6 for 20–30 minutes. Grate cheese on the top to serve.

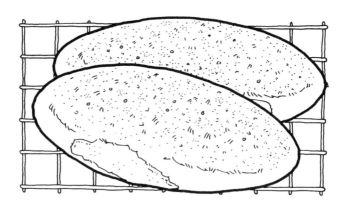

OLD LEIGH COOKIES

A visit to the cocklesheds at Leigh-on-Sea is always a memorable occasion. These cookies are meant to capture that experience.

Ingredients	Metric	Imperial	American
Butter	225g	8oz	1 cup
Soft brown sugar	400g	14oz	2 cups
Large egg	1	1	1
Vanilla essence	Few drops	Few drops	Few drops
Wholemeal flour	450g	1lb	4 cups
Desiccated coconut	75g	3oz	¼ cup
Glace cherries, chopped	50g	2oz	¼ cup

1. Cream the butter and sugar together until light. Beat the egg and the vanilla essence. Fold in the flour, coconut and chopped cherries until well distributed.

2. Roll out into a long sausage shape and refrigerate until hard. Cut into round biscuits and place on to greased baking trays. Bake at 190°/375°F/Gas Mark 5 until golden brown. Cool before eating.

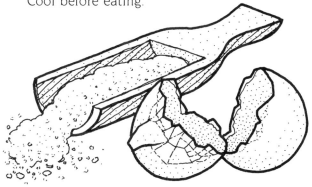

CASHEW NUT LOAF

Ingredients	Metric	Imperial	American
Ground cashew nuts	225g	8oz	2 cups
Fresh wholemeal breadcrumbs	100g	4oz	1 cup
Butter or margarine	25g	1oz	2 tbsp
Large onion, peeled and finely chopped	1	1	1
Garlic cloves, peeled and crushed	2	2	2
Egg whites	2	2	2
Egg yolk	1	1	1
Milk	150ml	¼ pint	½ cup
Lemon, grated rind	1	1	1
Dried, mixed herbs	1	1	1
Sea salt and black pepper			

Filling

	Metric	Imperial	American
Mushrooms, chopped	225g	8oz	1 cup
Butter or margarine	25g	1oz	2 tbsp
Egg yolk	1	1	1
Fresh wholemeal breadcrumbs	100g	4oz	1 cup
Yeast extract	1 tsp	1 tsp	1 tsp

1. Combine the nuts and breadcrumbs together in a mixing bowl.

2. Melt the butter in a pan, add the onion and garlic and fry until soft but not browned. Remove from the pan and add to the nut and crumb mixture.

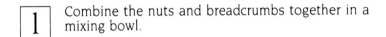

3 Beat the egg whites and egg yolk with the milk, lemon rind, herbs and add seasoning to taste. Pour into the nut and crumb mixture and mix thoroughly.

4 To make the filling: fry the mushrooms in the butter until soft. Stir in all the remaining ingredients and season.

5 Grease a 900g (2lb) loaf tin with butter, then press in half the nut mixture. Spread the filling mixture on top, then cover with the remaining nut mixture.

6 Cover with foil and bake in a preheated moderate oven, 180°C/350°F/Gas Mark 4 for 1 hour. When cooked, remove the loaf from the oven and let it stand for 10 minutes before turning it out. Serve hot or cold.

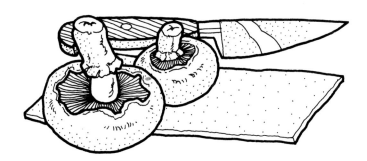

PIZZA

Ingredients	Metric	Imperial	American
Wholemeal flour	225g	8oz	2 cups
Sea salt	½ tsp	½ tsp	½ tsp
Fresh yeast	15g	½ oz	1 tsp
Warm water	150ml	¼ pint	½ cup
Topping			
Olive oil	1 tbsp	1 tbsp	1 tbsp
Medium onion, chopped	1	1	1
Clove of garlic, peeled and chopped	1	1	1
Tomatoes, skinned and chopped	1 lb	450g	1 lb
Tomato purée	2 tbsp	2 tbsp	2 tbsp
Oregano	1 tsp	1 tsp	1 tsp
Sea salt and freshly ground black pepper			
Mushrooms, sliced	100g	4oz	1 cup
Green pepper, cored, seeded and cut into 2 cm(1 in) strips	1	1	1
Mozzarella cheese, thinly sliced	100g	4oz	½ cup

1. Mix the flour and salt together in a bowl. Cream the yeast with a little of the water and leave until frothy. Add to the flour with the remaining water and the oil and mix to a soft dough.

2. Turn on to a floured surface and knead for 10 minutes until smooth and elastic. Place dough in a greased bowl and cover with oiled polythene. Leave in a warm place for about 1½ hours, until dough has doubled in size.

| 3 | Meanwhile, prepare tomato sauce for topping. Heat the oil in a pan, add the onion and garlic and fry for about 2 minutes. Add the tomatoes, puree, oregano, and salt and pepper to taste. Simmer for 10–15 minutes. The sauce should be quite thick and pulpy. |

| 4 | Turn the dough on to floured surface and knead for a few minutes. Divide in half and roll each piece out to a 20cm (8in) circle. |

| 5 | Cover within 1cm (½in) of edge with tomato sauce. Sprinkle chopped pepper and mushrooms on top and arrange the cheese slices over them. Season and leave to prove in a warm place for 15 minutes. |

| 6 | Bake in a preheated oven at 220°C/425°F/Gas Mark 7 for 25–30 minutes or until the dough is just firm to the touch and the cheese has melted. |

HOME-MADE MUESLI

Many shop-bought mueslis are full of sugar which provides calories without any nutrients. This is a basic muesli mixture to which you can add more dried or fresh fruit, and eat with unsweetened fruit juice, milk or natural yoghurt, it stores well in an airtight container.

Ingredients	Metric	Imperial	American
Rolled oats	500g	1¼lb	5 cups
Wheat flakes	100g	4oz	½ cup
Bran	75g	3oz	⅓ cup
Raisins	75g	3oz	⅓ cup
Sultanas	75g	3oz	⅓ cup
Mixed nuts, chopped	50g	2oz	⅓ cup
Demerara sugar	50g	2oz	6 tbsp
Skimmed milk powder	50g	2oz	4 tbsp

Mix all the ingredients thoroughly. Store in an airtight container.

WHOLEMEAL CHEESE TART

Ingredients	Metric	Imperial	American
Wholemeal pastry	450g	1 lb	1 lb
Filling			
Apples, peeled, cored and cooked	8	8	8
Cheese, grated	100g	4oz	½ cup
Nutmeg	Pinch	Pinch	Pinch
Topping			
Wholemeal flour	100g	4oz	½ cup
Brown sugar	100g	4oz	¼ cup
Almonds, roasted and chopped	50g	2oz	4 tbsp
Sunflower seeds	2 tbsp	2 tbsp	2 tbsp
Vegetable margarine	75g	3oz	¼ cup

1 Mix together the filling ingredients

Blend together the apples and cheese and add the nutmeg. Line a 15cm/6in pie dish with the pastry and pour in this filling mixture until ¾ full.

2 Mix together the dry topping ingredients and melt the margarine and pour this on to the filling

Mix together the dry topping ingredients. Melt the margarine and mix this in to form a crumbly texture. Refrigerate before sprinkling over the filling.

3 Bake for 25 minutes at 200°C/400°F/Gas Mark 6. When cool sprinkle with Demerara sugar to serve.

INDEX